The Principles of International Tax – A Multinational Perspective

The Principles of International Tax

A Multinational Perspective

Adrian Ogley

INTERFISC PUBLISHING

Published by Interfisc Publishing*
7 Chelverton Road
High Street, Putney
London SW15 1RN
United Kingdom

ISBN 0 9520442 0 X

Neither the author nor the publisher can accept responsibility for any loss occasioned to any person who either acts or refrains from action as a result of any statement contained in this book.

Before entering into a transaction, it is essential to obtain specific advice in relation to it.

British Library Cataloguing-in-Publication Data.
A catalogue record for this book is available from the British Library.

Typesetting by
Hewer Text Composition Services, Edinburgh, Scotland
and printed and bound by
Athenaeum Press Ltd., Newcastle upon Tyne, England.

(*Interfisc Publishing is a division of Interfisc Ltd)

Contents

Foreword

A glance back over thirty years' experience of international tax practice reveals many changes. We have come a long way from the days when professional firms would say 'we don't need anyone to specialise in international tax – we have offices in 80 countries', but genuine international practitioners are still only numbered in the hundreds worldwide. The art of finding optimum solutions within a host of apparently mutually contradictory constraints needs an approach which goes far beyond the sum of a knowledge of the tax systems of the countries concerned.

The nature of the work has also changed. In the old days, the typical client was a parent company with a range of operating subsidiaries whose management was astonished and delighted to find that there were more fiscally efficient, but still fairly simple, ways of setting up its structure. Today's financial markets are far more international and the real fun is to be had with sophisticated financial instruments and hedging techniques, and with cross-border mergers. In the latter case, one problem for tax advisers is often to persuade the gung-ho deals merchants to slow down just for a few days so we can get the tax planning right. Only too often they don't, and another few million accrues unnecessarily to the ungrateful tax collectors of this world.

Contrary to popular superstition, the serious end of the international tax profession is not and never has been concerned primarily with aggressive tax avoidance using tax havens, transfer pricing, and double-dipping, although these are the icing on the cake. The real problems come when a company, perfectly prepared to be a good corporate citizen of all the countries in which it operates, finds that their requirements mutually conflict. The adviser has to pick his way through a minefield to avoid being taxed more than once on the same profit. Over the years, the opportunity for avoidance has been seriously constrained by legislation. The corollary is that the task of the adviser has been made more challenging by the need to navigate essentially straightforward transactions though traps set up to catch those whose intentions were less innocent.

In 1974 I published my own book on international tax planning which readers seem to have found useful for far longer than its expected shelf life of two or three years. Having never, somehow, managed to produce another edition, I am delighted that my old friend, Adrian Ogley, has taken up the challenge with this excellent general study. It is a big subject and his book inevitably does not claim to contain all the answers. At least his readers, and there should be many of them, will know what questions to ask and will appreciate the richness, diversity and challenge of this fascinating subject.

John Chown
J.F. Chown & Company Limited
51 Lafone Street
London SE1 2LX

Preface

Now that international tax has become an accepted discipline in its own right, there is a clear need for a work of synthesis which strips away the mystique surrounding the subject and explains its basic principles in terms which a finance director, without a specialist tax background, will understand. Apart from finance directors, this book is intended for students of international tax, as well as practitioners embarking on their career and those who may not have had the time to 'stand back' from their work and to define fully the intellectual framework for what, until now, he or she may have been doing instinctively.

The multinational perspective, to which reference is made in the title, means that this book is concerned exclusively with international tax in so far as it affects multinational companies (and not individuals). It also means that the author has sought to adopt a multinational perspective in considering the issues involved in international tax, as opposed simply to considering these in the light of the tax legislation of one particular, national regime. Although the author's background, practical experience and reading will inevitably reveal a cultural bias, it is hoped that this has not detracted from the achievement of this wider aim.

So far as the structure of this work is concerned, it is divided into two distinct parts. After the introductory chapter, Part I of the book deals with the principal types of tax system and their interaction, with special emphasis on the question of double taxation at the shareholder level. There then follows a chapter entitled 'Double taxation and double tax agreements', which deals with the double taxation of profits accruing within companies and explains how double tax agreements seek to avoid, or at least mitigate this.

The proposals for harmonising direct, corporate taxes in Europe are then considered, with particular reference to the choice of tax system. The chapter on stapled stocks and hybrid structures explores innovative structures which have been devised by a number of multinationals to overcome the problem of double (or multiple) taxation of shareholders which would otherwise arise as a result of the inherent incompatibility of tax systems; this problem is either not addressed or inadequately addressed by the majority of double tax agreements.

Part II deals with the principles of international tax planning. The objectives of international tax planning have been described as the diversion, extraction and distribution of profits from high to low tax jurisdictions. Tax havens, by their very nature, offer the ultimate low-tax refuge for profits and accordingly a separate chapter outlines their attributes as well as their uses and abuses. Because the selection of the most appropriate means of finance is a fundamental means of tax planning, a separate chapter is devoted to the role of international financing and overseas finance companies. This is followed by a chapter describing certain specific corporate vehicles which are used for the diversion or extraction of profits, ie licensing, captive insurance and other service companies. The distribution of profits is dealt with in a chapter on the function and location of holding companies. A chapter on the Netherlands and Netherlands Antilles in international tax planning explores not only those features of the Dutch tax system which have made it a focal point in international tax planning, but also its interaction with the tax system of the Netherlands Antilles. However, no book on this subject would be complete without outlining the rapid growth of anti-avoidance measures in the international arena.

As some readers may prefer to dip into the book, as opposed to reading it from cover to cover, individual chapters are largely self-contained in their treatment of the topic under consideration. Where there are cross-references to other chapters, these simply serve to direct the reader to another part of the text where the same subject matter is dealt with in greater depth.

Because this book is a work of synthesis, it is difficult always to give credit where it is due. However, the author would like to acknowledge his particular indebtedness to John Chown, whose *Taxation and Multinational Enterprises* served as the model on which this book is based. Particular thanks are also due to Malcolm Gammie, a tax partner of Linklaters & Paines, and John Dewhurst, a director of J.F. Chown & Company Limited, who kindly read and commented on parts of the text, and in so doing suggested a number of improvements to it. Any errors, no doubt in parts of the text which did not benefit from this generosity, remain the sole responsibility of the author. The bibliography at the end of this book provides an indication of some of the many others who have contributed indirectly to this work.

It is simply not possible for a book of this kind to be completely up to date at the time of publication. Where specific features of a tax system are referred to, this is to illustrate either a point of principle or the variety of approaches which can be adopted by different jurisdictions to address the same issue. Furthermore, the references in Chapter 3 are to the OECD Model Double Taxation Convention of 1977, which will be familiar to practitioners. However, this has recently been revised and published as the 1992 Model Tax Convention on Income and Capital. In addition, the full text of the Ruding report has now been published.

It is hoped that additional material (for example, a chapter on international remuneration packages) can be incorporated in future editions of this book. Readers' suggestions for such additional material or for improvements to the existing text are welcome and should be addressed to:

Adrian Ogley
9 Lifford Street
LONDON SW15 1NY

1
Introduction

The study of international tax involves understanding how tax systems interact either when cross-border investment occurs or when there is a flow of funds, in some other form, between two or more countries. Where a company engages in cross-border investment, the country in which it is resident (the home country) may seek to tax profits arising from the overseas country (the host country) in which the investment has been made. As the host country will invariably seek to tax profits arising from a source within it, this would give rise to double taxation which, in the absence of provisions to prevent it, would deter or, at least, inhibit cross-border investment. This problem of double taxation would also arise where a resident of one country owns overseas income-producing property (of whatever description), or performs services in an overseas country which treats such income as having a domestic source, in which case both the country of residence and the country of source may seek to tax the same income. Capital gains arising in respect of overseas property may similarly give rise to double taxation.

The issue of double taxation has been recognised as a problem since medieval times, when there are recorded instances of it affecting individuals who lived in border areas and owned property on the other side of the border, and, as a consequence, were subject to tax in respect of the property in both the country in which they were resident and the country in which the property was located. However, it was only towards the end of the nineteenth century that it became an issue of more general concern, not only for the new imperial powers and their colonies but also for the newly formed federations, such as Switzerland with its constitution of 1874 and the new Germany with its federal laws of 1870, where the principal concern was double taxation arising as a result of the interaction of state taxes.

With the growth in international trade during the course of this century, the problem of double taxation became even more pressing. Between the two World Wars, it was the subject of a number of technical studies by the predecessor organisation of the League of Nations, the League itself and successor organisations. After the Second World War, the Organisation for Economic Co-operation and Development (OECD) published its first model double tax convention, in 1963. This was followed, in 1977, by the OECD's updated model double tax convention which exerted a significant influence on subsequent treaty negotiations by enabling them to take place in accordance with broadly pre-agreed parameters. In this way it contributed significantly to the extension of the network of double tax agreements and so helped both to promote and sustain the growth in international trade.

Fundamental to the problem of double taxation are the questions of the overall ceiling on the burden of tax to which an investor is to be exposed and how the total tax take is to be shared between the revenue authorities of the countries concerned. Double tax agreements set out the basis on which the treaty partner countries have agreed to resolve these issues. So far as concerns the ceiling for an investor's tax liability, this is often determined by reference to the higher of the two liabilities; either that of the investor's home country, or alternatively that of the host country. However, some countries fix this ceiling solely by reference to the rate of tax applying in the host country.

Turning to the question of the allocation of the tax take between the two countries, because the issue of double tax arose principally in capital exporting countries, it was in these countries that it became the subject of academic study which, as a rule, gave precedence to the taxing rights of the home country (ie, the capital exporting country or country of residence) over those of the country of source. This bias was reflected, to a greater or lesser extent, in the model double tax conventions which the various international organisations drew up. However, in order to redress this imbalance, in 1980 the United Nations issued its Model Double Taxation Convention between Developed and Developing Countries. This convention sought to give the host country (the country of source) the primary taxing rights.

Although the attention of early practitioners focused largely on the potential problems of double taxation, the development of extensive treaty networks helped not only to allay practitioners' concerns about double taxation but also to concentrate their attention on the opportunities for arbitraging between tax jurisdictions which international activity presents. These opportunities arise because multinationals have an advantage over a purely domestic company in that they can choose to locate production or some other activity in a country with a lower overall cost structure because the country in question imposes a lesser burden of taxation on such activity. The effective rate of tax, and hence the overall cost structure, often can be reduced further by diverting, extracting and distributing profits from these countries to jurisdictions with an even lower rate of tax, notably tax havens. The existence of treaty networks facilitates this process.

Connecting factors and liability to tax

Liability to tax in a particular country will arise where a company is resident or has some other form of presence, such as a branch or agent, in minimise direct taxes by fixing artificial transfer prices is the possible knock-on effect which this could have on indirect taxes. Although high prices charged to a subsidiary for components produced elsewhere in the group would reduce the subsidiary's profits, such a strategy may be self-defeating if the high prices charged result in increased duties which the subsidiary has to absorb. Alternatively, artificially low prices may lead to anti-dumping investigations. Exchange control considerations will also be a relevant factor in determining transfer prices.

In reality, the transfer pricing arrangements of the majority of multinationals have evolved, as the businesses have grown either organically or by acquisition, in response to a number of competing and often conflicting commercial considerations. The minimisation of direct taxes is only one such consideration. Although there is no doubt that a strategically defined and coherent transfer pricing policy can result in considerable savings in direct taxes, where transfer pricing arrangements have simply evolved in response to circumstances, it is unlikely to be possible to impose, after the event, a coherent and logical policy on a group. The imposition of such a policy, and the adjustment in price levels which this may entail, would not only cause considerable problems of morale but would also provoke suspicion on the part of the relevant revenue authorities. Accordingly, transfer pricing policy needs to be addressed at a strategic level at the outset, when a new business is being set up or product created.

The method of financing an overseas subsidiary will affect the amount of profits arising in the country concerned. Where, for example, an overseas subsidiary is financed largely by capital, this will have the effect of creating an endowment profit by increasing interest income, or reducing interest costs which would otherwise have been incurred. The endowment profit which accrues to the overseas subsidiary will be matched by a corresponding reduction in interest income or increase in interest expense in the country in which the immediate parent company is based. In order to prevent this shifting of taxable profits out of their jurisdiction, a number of countries deny interest relief for funds which are used to finance overseas investment in this way. However, restrictions which apply to interest relief are unlikely to prevent such a shifting of profits if the capital injected into the overseas subsidiary does not represent borrowed funds and it is for this reason that a number of countries have introduced administrative or regulatory controls governing the formation and capitalisation of overseas subsidiaries.

The extraction of profits

Where it is not possible to divert profits from high to low tax jurisdictions at the outset, the emphasis of international tax planning will be on extracting profits from high tax jurisdictions in a tax-deductible form. The term extraction of profits is used very loosely to include ensuring that overseas subsidiaries bear their share of centrally incurred overhead expenses through management charges. Whereas US multinationals often have very strictly defined policies for recharging these expenses, UK multinationals have tended to adopt a far less disciplined approach to this issue. Where this is the case, it is difficult to make good the neglect of the past by recharging such expenses in the future as this may provoke challenge from overseas revenue authorities, minority shareholders and local management, whose profit-sharing schemes may be adversely affected. The same principles will apply to the charging of technical service fees, although these relate to specific costs, unlike general overhead expenses.

In the same way that a subsidiary in a low tax jurisdiction will tend to be heavily capitalised, a subsidiary in a high tax country will tend to be thinly capitalised so that it is financed so far as possible by borrowings in respect of which the interest expense is tax deductible. However, it is common for countries to deny relief for interest expenses where a subsidiary is considered to be thinly capitalised. In these circumstances, the borrowings may be treated as akin to capital. This will be a particular risk where the borrowings are inter-group borrowings, although this risk may extend to external borrowings especially where these have been guaranteed by the parent or other group company. Where a subsidiary's borrowings are external to the group and unsupported by guarantees, it will invariably be harder for revenue authorities to treat the borrowings as capital and, as a consequence, to deny interest relief. However, some countries may apply an objective criterion, such as a maximum debt: equity ratio of 2:1, to determine whether a company is under-capitalised.

Other means of extracting profits from overseas companies are through licensing or royalty fees, rents and insurance premium payments. Such payments, including interest but with the exception of insurance premium payments, are likely to attract withholding taxes in the country of source. Where the country in question has entered into any double tax agreements, these are likely to eliminate or reduce the rate of withholding tax applying to payments made to a resident of the treaty partner. Where the potential beneficiary of such income is resident in a country which either has not entered into a double tax agreement or has concluded an agreement on less favourable terms than some other country, the practice of treaty shopping has developed. This involves the potential beneficiary structuring his affairs so that any payment is routed through the country with the most favourable treaty in order to minimise withholding taxes. However, there are a variety of anti-avoidance measures aimed at preventing this practice and the terms of a number of double tax agreements provide that if the tax authorities consider the payment to be excessive, they may treat it as a deemed distribution and not only impose withholding taxes but also deny relief for the payment.

Distributions

Where profits can neither be diverted nor extracted from high to low tax countries, they will inevitably accrue within them. In order to enable profits which accrue within a country to be distributed at as low a tax cost as possible, the investing company should have structured its investment at the outset with a view to achieving this. Because the double tax agreement (DTA) between the home and the host country may not provide for as large a reduction in the rate of withholding tax on dividends as the agreement between the host country and some third country, treaty shopping is a common feature in structuring outward investment. Treaty shopping in these circumstances will take the form of ownership of the investment through an intermediate holding company based in a third country.

Apart from obtaining the benefit of reduced rates of withholding tax on dividends, there are often domestic tax reasons why overseas investments should be held through a company based in a third country. These include the desire:

(1) to avoid or defer tax which would otherwise arise in the home country when dividends are distributed directly to it;
(2) to maximise double tax relief or foreign tax credits by converting income from a variety of different sources into income from a new, single source (that of the jurisdiction of the intermediate holding company) so that the rates of underlying tax can be averaged and so fully absorbed in the home country; or
(3) to avoid or defer tax in respect of any capital gain which would otherwise arise in the event of the sale of the overseas subsidiary(ies).

Once the appropriate structure is in place, profits should be distributed so far as possible out of high tax jurisdictions. This is especially so where the profits can be distributed by way of dividends without either attracting any withholding tax on payment or incurring any tax liability in either the home country or any intermediate jurisdiction. In such ideal circumstances, the increase in future profits or the reduction in financing costs arising from the distributed funds will accrue outside the high tax country and, by the same token, the high tax country will suffer a corresponding increase in financing costs or reduction in interest income.

Where, on the other hand, a dividend attracts a tax liability, whether a withholding tax in the country of source or a liability elsewhere, the future tax savings, resulting from the fact that profits will have been shifted out of a high tax country, should be offset against this in evaluating the desirability of taking a dividend. However, bearing in mind that the full amount of any dividend is likely to attract a tax cost (even if only a withholding tax at the rate of 5 per cent), whereas any tax saving will only relate to future income arising out of the funds used for the dividend, in such circumstances factors other than tax considerations are likely to influence dividend policy. Such factors would include the need for reserves at the parent company level and considerations relating to political or exchange risks associated with retaining profits in the host country.

Growth in tax havens

Improvements in communications and the speed of modern travel have enabled a number of small countries to develop the financial sectors of their economies by offering foreign investors the benefit of reduced or even nil rates of tax. Over the past 30 years, there has been a significant increase in the number of tax havens and in the levels of investment in their economies. The majority of tax havens have either been former British colonies or are British dependent territories. Such tax havens have provided shelter from the high rates of tax prevailing in developed countries during this period and consequently have acted as a staging post for profits which have been diverted, extracted or distributed from high tax jurisdictions.

International acquisitions and disposals

Structuring international acquisitions and disposals will be a principal focus of tax planning. In the case of acquisitions, the structure put in place at the outset will affect, possibly for a long time into the future, the tax charge which dividends and other cross-border flows of funds attract.

In the case of disposals, these may attract significant tax liabilities in either all, or a combination, of the country of source, the country of residence of the parent company or some intermediate jurisdiction. As these tax liabilities could significantly erode the proceeds of sale, the principal focus of tax planning in this area will be to minimise tax liabilities arising in any jurisdiction and to maximise the offset of any tax liabilities incurred 'down the line' so as to avoid double taxation (or worse). Apart from the fact that an international disposal will give rise to a capital receipt which is likely to attract, at least, one tax liability, it may be possible by careful tax planning to influence where the net proceeds of disposal are received. If these are received in a low tax country, they may be able to compound at a low (or even nil) rate of tax in the future.

International and domestic tax planning

Where an international acquisition is contemplated, it is essential that the group tax manager has a detailed knowledge of the rules governing the taxation of outward investment in his home country. He should also know how these general principles are modified by the particular circumstances of his own group.

The group's professional advisers or the tax manager's opposite number(s) in the country(ies) in which the target(s) is(are) based should have a detailed knowledge of how best to structure inward investment into the jurisdiction(s) in question.

After initial consultation between the head office and the overseas tax advisers, it should be possible to formulate, in outline terms, a preferred structure for effecting an acquisition. This structure is likely to involve:

(1) determining the most appropriate method of financing the acquisition;
(2) deciding on the form which both the acquisition and the consideration should take. This will include considering whether the acquisition should be of assets or shares and the extent to which it should be 'unbundled' and broken down into constituent elements;
(3) deciding how the consideration should be attributed; and
(4) choosing an appropriate vehicle for the acquisition.

Where possible, a detailed review of the target company(ies) or group'(s) tax profile should be undertaken in order to determine whether or to what extent it will be necessary or desirable to modify any initial outline structure to take account of the particular tax profile of the target.

Although it is widely appreciated at a domestic level that there will be a conflict between the interests of an acquirer and those of a vendor, it is not so widely appreciated that the situation will be broadly similar at an international level. Success in any negotiation will depend on preparation, bargaining power, skill, and patience. Patience (and time) is essential in this process because it will allow the parties concerned to identify those areas where their particular circumstances may reduce or eliminate what would otherwise be a conflict of interest and allow both parties to come away from the negotiating process with that elusive something for nothing.

In the case of international disposals, the same broad considerations will apply, except from the opposite perspective. In these circumstances, the focus will be on avoiding or minimising any tax liability in the country of source at the preliminary stage. Once this has been achieved, the focus will switch to tax planning in relation to the home and/or intermediate country and minimising any tax liability arising there, while at the same time, maximising the offset of any tax suffered in the country of source.

In the absence of international acquisitions or disposals, routine tax planning in relation to overseas investments will be the province of local management who should ensure that they are complying with domestic requirements while, at the same time, minimising domestic taxes. The parent company's tax manager will simply have a 'watching brief' to ensure that there are no changes in commercial circumstances or proposed changes in legislation which may make it desirable to restructure investments in a particular jurisdiction. However, it should be borne in mind that activities which appear to be purely domestic can have wider implications. As an example of this, the merger of overseas subsidiaries of a UK group (usually undertaken for domestic tax or commercial reasons in the country of operation) will have the effect of eliminating any credit in the UK for underlying taxes which would otherwise attach to the retained profits of the merging company up to the date of merger. Thus an apparently domestic transaction (the merger of local subsidiary companies) will have unforeseen international ramifications. Accordingly it is important to ensure that local management are aware of the type of domestic transaction which has an international dimension, so that they can involve the head office tax function in this aspect of their tax planning.

Growth in anti-avoidance measures

Although the principles of international tax planning appear straightforward, the practice is invariably complex. This complexity lies in the specific features of individual tax regimes and has been aggravated by the recent growth in anti-avoidance legislation.

In general, anti-avoidance legislation can be divided into the following categories:

(1) legislation aimed at preventing either the migration of companies, or the shifting of profits into low tax jurisdictions by restricting a company's ability either to form, or alternatively to introduce capital into, overseas subsidiaries based in such jurisdictions. Anti-avoidance legislation of this kind often takes the form of a requirement for an administrative consent which may be linked in some way to exchange controls;

(2) legislation aimed at preventing the avoidance or deferral of tax by hoarding profits in overseas low tax jurisdictions. The majority of capital exporting countries have legislation of this kind, eg US sub-Part 'F' legislation and the UK's controlled foreign company legislation;

(3) legislation aimed at preventing the manipulation of profits through artificial transfer pricing. This type of legislation is common to both capital exporting and importing countries. In addition, most countries have legislation aimed at preventing the extraction of profits through excessive charges, such as royalty or interest payments. Such legislation will often deem such payments to have been hidden distributions and accordingly subject them not only to corporation tax but also to withholding tax;

(4) legislation aimed at preventing treaty shopping. This may range from specific anti-treaty shopping provisions, which are incorporated into treaties themselves, aimed at curbing defined abuses to general

limitation of benefit clauses. In addition, certain countries refuse to apply the provisions of a double tax agreement where it runs counter to provisions of their domestic legislation. This concept of treaty override has been taken to such extremes by the US that it threatens to undermine the value of any double tax agreement between it and other countries.

Summary

The growth in international trade which occurred in the post-war period was sustained and promoted by the development of networks of double tax agreements. Simultaneous progress in the fields of transport and communication not only stimulated international trade but also encouraged the development and use of tax havens because even the most remote location became accessible. This improvement in communications also helped to spread information about tax planning techniques from jurisdiction to jurisdiction. This, in turn, led tax authorities to take retaliatory action to protect their domestic tax bases and to quicken the speed of their response.

Part I

Structural issues: tax systems, the shareholder and double taxation

2

Tax Systems and their Interaction

The purpose of this chapter is to outline, in general terms, the ways in which the tax regime in an investor's home country may interact with that of a prospective host country. Understanding this interaction is essential in order to be able to evaluate properly any investment proposal.

Incompatibility of tax systems and policies

The majority of developed countries have, since the end of the Second World War, adopted a policy of progressively liberalising trade and international investment. Just as the barriers of exchange controls have been reduced or removed, so too have the fiscal constraints on overseas investment. However, this process of liberalisation has stopped short of addressing the fundamental distortions which arise as a result of the inherent incompatibility of differing tax systems. This issue has been brought sharply into focus by the debate on tax harmonisation in the context of the European Single Market.

Apart from the possible incompatibility of systems of direct taxation, another incompatibility lies in the tax policies which governments pursue. In particular, the differing extent to which they rely on indirect or other forms of taxation, apart from direct taxes on business profits, as a means of raising revenue.

Direct and indirect taxation

Where a host government raises revenue through indirect taxes such as taxes on consumption or equally through direct payroll-related taxes and social security levies, this will have the effect of increasing business costs, and as a consequence will reduce *before* tax profits. On the other hand, where direct taxes are levied on business profits, this will have the effect of reducing *after* tax profits. This is illustrated in the examples below which compare the position on the assumptions that:

in example (a) profits are subject to direct taxes at the rate of 50 per cent.

in example (b) no direct taxes are levied on business profits. Instead government revenue is raised by indirect taxes which increase costs by an amount equal to the direct taxes in (a).

	Example (a)	*Example (b)*
Turnover	1,000	1,000
Costs	800	900
Profit before tax	200	100
Less direct taxes 50%	100	–
Profit after tax	100	100

Although *before* tax profits in example (a) are double those in example (b), the net of tax returns are the same in both examples. This illustrates the importance of comparing net of tax returns when appraising any potential investment.

Taxation of shareholders and corporate profits

The fundamental issue at the heart of any tax system is the extent to which the principle of double taxation is accepted as part of the logic of the system or alternatively the extent to which the tax system tries to integrate, fully or in part, the tax liability of the company with the personal tax liability of the shareholder. Different tax systems adopt differing approaches to this issue.

At one extreme, a company is treated as an entirely separate entity, distinct from its shareholders. Its profits are taxed within the company and then, on distribution, the same profits are taxed in the hands of shareholders. This double taxation of corporate profits lies at the heart of the so-called classical system. However, certain jurisdictions which have adopted a classical tax system nevertheless incorporate provisions in their legislation to eliminate one layer of taxation in the case of certain categories of company, usually small or family companies. The rationale behind these provisions is that such companies should be allowed to enjoy the commercial benefits of incorporation without suffering the fiscal disadvantage of double taxation which might act otherwise as a deterrent to incorporation and hence discourage enterprise. In the US, the 'Sub-Chapter S' corporation provides such fiscal transparency and allows the shareholders to be taxed as if they were a partnership. However, the US restricts the benefit of these provisions to companies which have less than 35 shareholders, are not listed, and do not have any foreign shareholders. Most other jurisdictions which have relieving provisions of this kind similarly restrict the categories of company to which they apply. In Australia, before the introduction of the imputation system, the domestic tax legislation contained no such relieving provision. As a consequence, there were attempts to overcome, through the use of trading trusts, the problem of double taxation while at the same time obtaining the benefit of the corporate form. This was achieved by trading through a trust with a corporate trustee. Under this arrangement, profits accrued directly to the individual beneficiaries and were taxed in their hands accordingly, while the corporate trustee afforded the individual beneficiaries protection from the risks associated with unlimited liability.

At the other extreme from the classical system, a full imputation system provides fiscal transparency because tax suffered at the corporate level is available in full as a tax credit to the shareholder on distribution of the profits. On the other hand, under a partial imputation system, a residual liability, which is not available as a tax credit to shareholders, attaches to corporate profits. In this respect the partial imputation system accepts by implication the same principle of double taxation which underlies the classical system. The UK, which has adopted a partial imputation system, nevertheless grants full imputation in the case of so-called small companies. There is in this respect a similarity between the full imputation granted to small companies in the UK and the concept of the US 'Sub-Chapter S' corporation although there are significant differences in the definitions of companies which qualify under the relevant legislation.

Turning now to a consideration of the most frequently encountered type of tax system (Appendix 1, column (i) shows which of these have been adopted by the principal jurisdictions), these are:

The classical system

Under this system, profits earned by companies are effectively taxed twice; once within the company, where they are subject to corporation or profits tax, and then again on distribution in the hands of shareholders (where they are subject to income tax). This double taxation of profits will generally extend to capital gains where these are subject to tax and the gain accrues within a company. So far as concerns the income tax liability of the shareholders, the company often acts as a collecting agent for the revenue authorities by withholding income tax at the standard rate from dividend payments. Where the shareholder's liability is above or below the standard rate, the revenue authorities either collect the additional liability by direct assessment or alternatively make a repayment.

Set out below is an example of the tax charges which arise under such a system:

Taxation of the company		
Profits		100
Corporation tax thereon @ 30%		30
Profits available for distribution		70
Dividend payment		
Distribution to shareholder		70
Income tax withheld at standard rate (say 25%)		17.50
Net amount paid to shareholder		52.50
Taxation of shareholder		
Dividend received (gross)		70
Tax at marginal rate of (say) 40%	28	28
Less income tax withheld	17.50	
Tax payable by direct assessment	10.50	
Net amount available to shareholder		42

Imputation system

There are, in general, two types of imputation system: the full and the partial imputation. Under both types of imputation system, a tax credit attaches (is 'imputed') to any dividend paid to shareholders. Under a full imputation system this tax credit will equal the appropriate proportion of tax suffered at the corporate level. On the other hand, under a partial imputation system the tax credit will represent part only of the tax suffered at the corporate level. Thus the tax liability under a full or partial imputation system is suffered at the corporate level and the shareholder obtains, on distribution of the profits, a full or partial credit in respect of this tax. Because, under an imputation system, tax is suffered at the corporate level, with the tax credit providing a mechanism for transferring the benefit of this tax to the shareholder, there is no withholding tax on dividends.

Set out below is an example showing a full and a partial imputation system which assumes a rate of personal tax of 25 per cent, in the case of both the full and the partial imputation system. In the case of the partial imputation system, a 33 per cent rate of corporation tax (the current UK rate) has been assumed.

	(I) Full imputation system		(II) Partial imputation system
Profit	100		100
Tax	25		33
Profits available for distribution	75		67
Dividend	75		67
Tax credit	25		22
Dividend inclusive of tax credit	100		89
Residual tax suffered at corporate level	–	(100-89)	11

Partial shareholder relief schemes

Partial shareholder relief schemes are similar in effect to partial imputation systems. These grant relief either in the form of a tax allowance of a fixed percentage in respect of domestic dividends received by resident shareholders or alternatively by applying a lower rate of tax to domestic dividend income. Japan has adopted such a tax system.

The split-rate and dividend deduction systems

Under the split-rate system, distributed profits are subject to a lower rate of tax than retained profits. The rationale for this is that distributed profits will be subject to additional tax on distribution (ie, income tax in the hands of the shareholder). The shareholder is liable to tax in respect of the grossed up dividend (grossed up by the tax credit and withholding taxes). Against this liability are set the tax credit and withholding taxes. On the other hand, the tax on retained profits is regarded as a final tax. Germany is the only major economy to have adopted a split-rate system. A dividend deduction system achieves a similar effect by granting a deduction in the calculation of a company's taxable profits for dividend distributions. Both systems will involve a withholding tax on dividends to ensure that the shareholders' personal tax liability is met, at least in part.

Implications of different tax systems at the domestic level

Where profits accruing to companies are subject to two incidences of tax, inevitably there is an incentive to try to avoid at least one such incidence.

This can be achieved by ensuring that companies are financed so far as possible by debt, as opposed to equity capital. Provided that payments of interest are allowed as a deduction in arriving at the taxable profits of a company and the corresponding receipt is subject to tax only in the hands of the recipient, only one charge to tax will arise in respect of that income. Accordingly classical tax systems tend to encourage high levels of debt financing in companies. This is considered by many economic commentators to be undesirable because the corporate sector becomes excessively geared and overdependent on debt financing. Apart from encouraging debt financing, a classical tax system will also encourage the extraction of profits from companies by way of other charges, such as high levels of remuneration for shareholder/directors. Classical tax systems invariably have anti-avoidance provisions aimed at preventing the extraction of profits by such arrangements. Where profits cannot be extracted, a classical tax system will encourage companies to retain profits so as to avoid the second incidence of tax, which arises on distribution. For this reason most classical tax systems have anti-avoidance provisions aimed at preventing companies from hoarding profits although such provisions are notoriously difficult to administer and enforce. This disincentive to distribute profits is economically undesirable because it may result in the retention of profits in businesses which generate below average returns. Where, on other hand, a significant proportion of corporate profits is distributed to shareholders, companies hoping to finance new investment will have to compete for funds in the open market where market forces will allocate these to those companies/investments which offer the prospect of above average returns.

In assessing the domestic implications of other types of tax system it is necessary to consider the extent of the integration of personal and corporate liabilities and of any difference between the maximum rate of personal and corporate tax.

In the case of either a full or partial imputation system, where the tax credit attaching to dividend distributions discharges the shareholder's liability to tax at the basic rate, the decision as to whether profits should be retained within the company or distributed to shareholders will be broadly neutral provided that the majority of shareholders are not subject to personal tax at rates significantly in excess of the tax credit.

Under the partial relief schemes, the principal considerations will be the extent of the allowances granted to shareholders in respect of domestic dividends and also the difference between the rate of personal and corporate tax.

Where the majority of shareholders are subject to a rate of income tax which is below the rate of corporation tax applying to retained profits, a split-rate system provides a positive incentive to distribute profits because such a system mitigates the overall burden of tax imposed on the distribution of profits, while at the same time penalising the retention of profits.

Where there is no difference between the maximum rate of personal tax and the rate of corporate tax, a dividend deduction system which allows full deductibility of distributions will be neutral as regards the retention or distribution of profits.

Residence of companies and the taxation of overseas income

Residence of companies

It is important to understand the concept of corporate residence (and by the same token what constitutes non-residence) especially as definitions tend to vary, depending on the jurisdiction. For example, the US, and more recently the UK, treat any company incorporated in their jurisdiction as resident for tax purposes. Where, on the other hand, a company is incorporated outside their jurisdiction, its residence status will be determined by reference to criteria other than the place of incorporation, such as the place where it is managed and controlled or effectively managed. Other jurisdictions do not have regard to a company's place of incorporation in order to determine its residence status. Ireland is an example of a jurisdiction which determines corporate residence exclusively by reference to the place in which the company is managed and controlled. As a consequence, it is possible to have a company which although incorporated in the Republic of Ireland, is not resident there for tax purposes.

The concept of management and control derives from case law in the UK and has been adopted as the test for corporate residence by a large number of other jurisdictions whose legal systems have been influenced by the English system and its precedents. Until recently, the UK revenue authorities regarded the concept of management and control as synonymous with the place of effective management (the definition contained in the OECD Model Double Taxation Convention 1977 and adopted in the majority of double tax treaties). However, the UK revenue authorities now accept that the two concepts are not in fact identical but have not defined the distinction between them. It is probably fair to say that because the term management and control stresses the importance of the place where board meetings are held, it places greater emphasis on the form than does the term effective management, which has regard to the substance of where responsibility lies for actual day-to-day operations.

Because of the variety of definitions of corporate residence, as well as the scope for differing interpretations of the facts of a particular case by the revenue authorities, it is possible for a company to be regarded as resident in two jurisdictions (dually resident). For this reason, the OECD Double Tax Convention contains a so-called 'tie-breaker' clause which states that where a company would otherwise be dually resident, it shall be regarded for the purpose of the relevant treaty as resident in that state in which it is effectively managed. However, not all double tax agreements contain such a clause. The UK/US double tax agreement is an example of a double tax agreement which does not include such a provision.

Taxation of overseas income

As a general rule, countries impose tax on the worldwide profits of resident companies while charging non-resident companies to tax only in respect of profits which arise from a source within their jurisdiction. Accordingly where a company is resident in one country but derives profits from a source within some other country (whether from a branch or whatever), both the investing company's country of residence and the source-country of the profits could claim, in principle, the right to tax those same profits. The resulting double taxation would reduce the returns from overseas investment so as, at worst, to discourage it completely or, at least, inhibit it severely.

Relief from double taxation

Tax systems commonly adopt one of two basic approaches in order to overcome or reduce the problem of double taxation which would otherwise arise where a company is engaged in business across borders. The first (and less common) approach involves the country of residence of the investor exempting from tax profits which arise outside its jurisdiction; the so-called exemption method. The second approach involves the investing company's country of residence giving relief for overseas taxes suffered by offset ('credit') of the foreign tax against the corresponding domestic liability; the so-called credit method. (For details of the approach adopted by the principal jurisdictions see Appendix 1, column (ii).) This relief may be granted either by virtue of the provisions of a double tax agreement (treaty relief) or unilaterally.

The territorial principle and the exemption method

The territorial principle involves the jurisdiction in which the investor resides voluntarily forgoing any taxing rights in relation to income arising outside its own jurisdiction. It does this by granting such income an exemption from tax. The exemption method has the advantage not only of avoiding the computational complexities of the 'credit' method, but also of preventing fiscal considerations from distorting an investor's choice of investment. This distortion arises under a system of worldwide taxation because dividends received from a host country which raises revenue through indirect taxes are subject to direct tax in full in the country of residence (ie, no effective credit is available for indirect taxes suffered).

Where the exemption method applies, on the other hand, an investor need only concern himself with the overseas tax suffered in relation to any overseas investment. Thus for tax planning purposes, the overseas tax liability will be the ultimate liability and the benefit of any tax incentive or of any overseas tax saving will remain intact when profits are eventually remitted to the investor's home country. The example on page 21 illustrates this and contrasts the position under the 'credit' method.

Worldwide taxation and the 'credit' method

The majority of countries impose tax on the worldwide profits of resident companies. Where this is the case and a company establishes an overseas branch, the profits of the branch will be subject to tax in both the overseas as well as the home country, with the latter granting relief for any direct overseas taxes suffered. By the same token, where an overseas branch incurs a loss, this will be available for offset against domestic, or other, taxable profits. Accordingly where the initial costs of overseas expansion result in losses, these are favourably treated under a system of worldwide taxation because immediate tax relief will be available. Because worldwide taxation offers this advantage, certain countries which apply an exemption system (notably France) have introduced special provisions to grant their residents an equivalent relief for such start-up losses. The provisions which grant this relief usually provide for its automatic recapture after a defined period. In the absence of provisions for the recapture of such losses, future profits of the branch would escape tax entirely where:

(1) they could be offset by losses carried forward in the overseas country; and
(2) they were not subject to tax in the home country by virtue of the application of the exemption method.

Although the worldwide profits of resident companies are taxed under a system of worldwide taxation, the profits (which accrue outside the jurisdiction in question) of non-resident subsidiaries are only subject to tax in the hands of the parent company when remitted by way of dividends or deemed dividends. This deferral is a fundamental feature of the system of worldwide taxation as it allows overseas resident subsidiaries to compete on an equal tax footing with either the overseas subsidiaries of multinationals based elsewhere or, where there is capital import neutrality, with locally owned companies.

Where the shareholding exceeds 10 per cent and dividends are remitted or deemed to have been remitted, these are grossed up by the amount of underlying tax and relief is granted in respect of underlying taxes suffered (in addition to relief for withholding taxes). The relief for underlying taxes may extend to taxes suffered by sub-subsidiaries throughout an extended chain of ownership. Until 1992, the Japanese tax system was notable in that it denied relief for the underlying taxes of second-tier subsidiaries.

The operation of a system of worldwide taxation may be illustrated by using the earlier example on page 13 and assuming that profits are distributed in full (without attracting any withholding taxes).

In example (a) profits are subject to direct taxes at the rate of 50 per cent.

In example (b) no direct taxes are levied on business profits. Instead government revenue is raised by indirect taxes which increase costs by an amount equal to the direct taxes in (a).

	Example (a)	*Example (b)*
Turnover	1,000	1,000
Costs	800	900
Profit before tax	200	100
Less direct taxes	100	–
Net profit – distributed in full	100	100

Where an exemption system applies, the distributed profits will represent the investor's net return.

Taxation of dividends in the hands of an overseas corporate shareholder subject to worldwide taxation:

	Example (a)		*Example (b)*	
Dividend (grossed up 100 + underlying tax 100)		200		100
Domestic tax (say 35%)	70		35	
Relief for underlying taxes	100	(100)	–	
Excess (unrelieved) overseas tax	30		–	
Domestic tax		–		(35)
Net profits available to shareholder		100		65

Example (a) illustrates how relief for overseas taxes may be restricted under a system of worldwide taxation where the overseas rate of tax exceeds the domestic rate of tax. Example (b) illustrates how a system of worldwide taxation discriminates against capital importing countries which raise revenue through indirect taxes because it provides no mechanism for giving effective relief for the indirect taxes so suffered. In addition, where a capital importing country in principle raises taxes through direct taxes but chooses to stimulate investment by offering a tax holiday, a system of worldwide taxation will confiscate the incentive when profits are repatriated.

There are essentially two bases on which relief for underlying taxes may be granted. Under the first basis, the relief is subject to specific limitation on a source by source basis, whereas under the second basis the foreign source income is pooled and is subject to an overall limitation. The UK, which has adopted the first basis, limits the credit for overseas tax to the corresponding UK tax attributable to that income. Thus the maximum liability in relation to each particular source of income will always be the higher of the UK or the overseas rate of tax. Where, on the other hand, an overall limitation applies, this may allow otherwise unrelieved overseas tax from one source to be offset against income from another overseas source which has suffered a lower rate of tax.

In countries such as the UK where relief for underlying taxes is subject to specific limitation, it may nevertheless be possible to achieve the benefits of an overall limitation method by routing dividends through an intermediate jurisdiction, so converting dividends with a multiplicity of underlying rates of tax into a dividend from a single source (the company in the intermediate jurisdiction) with an averaged underlying rate of tax. (This is illustrated in Chapter 10, *Holding Companies and Co-ordination Centres*.)

Overseas investment and interest relief

Although the majority of jurisdictions grant relief for interest incurred in making or acquiring domestic investments, only a minority grant full relief for interest incurred in making or acquiring an overseas investment. (See Appendix 1, column (iii).)

Those jurisdictions which grant relief undoubtedly do so to avoid discriminating against overseas investment. On the other hand, jurisdictions which deny relief in such circumstances invariably do so in order to prevent the erosion of their revenue base. This erosion would occur where the jurisdiction in question either grants exemption in respect of overseas income or allows relief for underlying taxes attributable to the overseas income and the underlying taxes would eliminate or substantially reduce any liability which would otherwise arise in the home country.

In the UK relief is available, in principle, for interest incurred in acquiring overseas investments. It is common practice to insulate this interest expense in a separate company from the company which owns the overseas investment and receives the dividends. By insulating the interest in this way, the overseas dividend income is available in full to absorb the attributable underlying tax. In the event that there is insufficient underlying tax fully to relieve the overseas income, the group relief provisions will enable so much of the interest expense as is either necessary or available to offset the overseas income so as to eliminate or reduce any residual (UK) liability.

The availability, in the UK, of interest relief for overseas investment, combined with the use of dual resident companies, enabled UK groups to structure their affairs so as to obtain interest relief in both the UK and the US. The dual resident company (resident in both the US and the UK and so forming part of both the US consolidated filing and the UK tax group) would incur the interest expense which would then be offset through the consolidated filing in the US and through the group relief provisions in the UK. This strategy was possible because the UK/US double tax agreement does not contain the usual 'tie-breaker' clause, contained in the OECD model convention, which provides that a company can be resident in only one or other of the countries which are parties to a double tax agreement and defines which one. However, anti-avoidance legislation was introduced in both the US and the UK to put an end to this practice.

Other jurisdictions are less generous than the UK with regard to the granting of interest relief for overseas investment. Although the US does not restrict interest relief per se, it does take interest into account in the 'source' formula for the calculation of relief for underlying taxes and this has the effect of restricting tax credit relief. In contrast, the Netherlands specifically disallows interest incurred in financing the acquisition of a foreign participation; this is on the basis that the income from such a participation is exempt from tax in the Netherlands. However, even where the legislation in a particular country denies interest relief in principle, it may still be possible in practice to obtain an element of relief because of the technical complexity of defining the precise purpose for which funds have been borrowed.

This problem can be illustrated by the example of a highly capitalised group with pre-existing, long-term borrowings and short-term surplus funds, which uses these funds together with additional borrowings to finance a substantial acquisition. In this example, the interest on the additional borrowings would clearly be disallowed but it would not be possible to determine whether the surplus funds represent part of the original capital or alternatively an element of the pre-existing, long-term borrowings of the group. This concept is often referred to as the 'fungibility' of capital. Tax systems which disallow interest incurred for the purpose of making overseas investments have developed their own conventions for attributing interest costs in these circumstances. Under these conventions, effective relief may be available for an element of the interest expense in such circumstances.

Interaction of classical and imputation systems at the international level

Because a classical system accepts the principle of double taxation, it distinguishes between the tax attributable to the source of corporate profits (ie, the corporate tax) and the tax attributable to the return on capital (ie, the dividend withholding tax and other taxation on the shareholder). This simplifies the process of negotiating double tax agreements because the capital exporting country has only to concern itself with rejecting entirely, or, at least, moderating the capital importing country's claim to a share of the tax levied on the return on capital, as represented by any dividend withholding tax. For this reason, under the terms of the majority of double tax agreements between developed countries, this withholding tax is generally reduced to 5 per cent where the shareholding is in excess of 25 per cent.

When received in the home country of the investing company, the dividend is either exempt from tax or, where a worldwide system of taxation applies, subject to tax with a credit for overseas taxes (including withholding taxes) suffered. On distribution of these overseas profits, the shareholders will incur a personal tax liability which will be met, in full or in part, by domestic tax withheld from the dividend. Thus under a classical system, there is no difference in the tax treatment applying to distributions of domestic or overseas profits.

By integrating the tax liability of the company with that of the shareholder, an imputation system creates additional complexity at the international level. This complexity affects both outward and inward investment.

Outward investment and the 'prejudice' problem

Most imputation systems contain provisions to ensure that a tax credit is available to a shareholder only where an equivalent amount of domestic tax has actually been paid. This is especially important to the UK revenue authorities as this tax credit is repayable, in whole or in part, to a wide range of organisations, in particular approved pension schemes and charities as well as to certain categories of individuals, including non-resident and resident individuals. The UK legislation ensures that this tax is actually paid by requiring companies to account for advance corporation tax (ACT) when paying a dividend.

This ACT may be offset against UK corporation tax otherwise payable. Accordingly where a company is in an overall tax-paying position in the

UK, the ACT simply represents a prepayment of tax. Where, on the other hand, the UK company paying the dividend has either too little or no UK corporation tax liability against which to offset the ACT, it will represent an additional tax cost and not merely a prepayment of tax.

This problem arises most commonly in the case of companies with insufficient UK source income. Although the rules under which ACT may be offset against any corporation tax liability are extremely flexible and allow companies to allocate and offset it in the first instance against current UK profits or, failing that, to carry it back against past UK profits or forward, indefinitely, against future profits, an increasing number of UK groups face the problem of irrecoverable ACT. This can be explained by:

(1) the historically high levels of overseas investment by UK groups;
(2) the relatively high levels of dividend payments by UK groups, compared with their international competitors;
(3) the erosion of the UK profit base which has been caused by the current deep recession;
(4) the reduction in the rate of corporation tax in recent years.

The arithmetic of an imputation system's in-built prejudice against overseas investment may be illustrated by comparing the amount of foreign source profits required to fund a dividend payment with the amount of UK source profits required to pay the same dividend. For the sake of the comparison, it has been assumed that the foreign source profits have attracted tax at the same rate as the current rate of corporation tax in the UK, ie 33 per cent.

	UK source	*Foreign source*
Pre-tax profits	1,120	1,493
Corporation tax @ 33%	370	493
	750	1000
Less: ACT written off	–	250
Dividend payment	£750	£750

It will be seen from the above example that it requires overseas profits of £1,493 in order to finance a dividend of £750, whereas it only requires UK source profits of £1,120 to finance the same dividend. The increase in profits required to finance a dividend paid out of foreign source profits is represented by additional overseas tax of £123 (at 33 per cent) and the ACT write-off of £250 and totals £373. It will be apparent from this example that although ACT is not a withholding tax from a legal standpoint, it has the same effect as a withholding tax where overseas source profits are being distributed.

Because this prejudice problem makes a country which has an imputation system unattractive as a location for an intermediate holding company (which by definition will be distributing foreign source income), France recently introduced reforms which exempt French holding companies from this equalisation tax where:

- two thirds or more of their assets consist of shareholdings of 10 per cent or more in foreign companies;
- two thirds of their income (excluding capital gains) derive from foreign shareholdings.

However, where no equalisation tax is paid, the shareholder is not entitled to the imputation credit. Although this reform provides little benefit for the resident shareholder, it will make France more attractive as a jurisdiction in which to locate intermediate holding companies.

Inward investment and the prejudice problem

In order to raise the same amount of revenue through an integrated system as is raised through a classical tax system with two incidences of tax, an imputation system must impose a higher rate of tax. That this is the case is evidenced by the fact that the UK increased its rate of corporation tax from 40 to 52 per cent when it adopted an imputation system in 1973.

In effect, the increase in the rate of tax under an imputation system was required to finance the tax credit to which resident shareholders became entitled. However, as non-resident shareholders do not benefit from this tax credit, it is argued that imputation systems discriminate against overseas investors. In order to meet these objections when negotiating double tax agreements the UK has been willing to concede a refund, of a proportion at least, of this tax credit to residents of the treaty partner country. However, because in many cases this refund does not flow directly to the non-resident shareholder, it may attract, indirectly, tax in the shareholder's country of residence or simply reduce the foreign tax credit otherwise available for offset and so not achieve the objective of putting non-resident shareholders in the same position as resident shareholders. This issue is discussed at greater length in Chapter 3: *Double Taxation and Double Tax Agreements.*

Conclusion

So far as concerns the basis on which overseas income is taxed, an exemption method not only avoids the computational complexities involved in calculating underlying rates of tax (and the attendant compliance costs), but also allows investment decisions to be based solely on an appraisal of the projected net of tax returns in the host country.

Unlike a system of worldwide taxation, an exemption method does not effectively confiscate tax incentives offered by a host country or discriminate against investment in a country which raises revenue by indirect, as opposed to direct, taxes.

So far as concerns tax systems, although imputation systems overcome the problem of double taxation at the domestic level, they exacerbate it at the international level. It remains to be seen whether the member states of the European Community will develop a satisfactory basis for overcoming this problem within the context of the EC which can then be adopted at a wider international level.

3
Double Taxation and Double Tax Agreements

The OECD Model Double Tax Convention defines double taxation as

> the imposition of comparable taxes in two (or more) states on the same taxpayer in respect of the same subject-matter and for identical periods.

How it arises

Most countries tax their residents on their worldwide income. Accordingly a company, resident in a country applying a system of worldwide taxation, will be faced with the problem of potential double taxation where it establishes an overseas branch. This is because the company's country of residence will tax its worldwide profits, including those accruing to the overseas branch, while the country in which the branch is located will invariably tax these same profits because they arise from a source within it. In the absence of any arrangements to prevent or relieve double taxation, the taxpayer would be faced with the dual claims, of his country of residence and the country of source, to tax the same branch profits.

Other forms of income, apart from business profits, can also give rise to double taxation; these include rents, royalties, pensions, remuneration and overseas capital gains.

Double tax agreements

Double tax agreements are often referred to as double tax treaties or conventions. As the name implies, the principal purpose of such an agreement is to eliminate double taxation by agreeing on an overall ceiling for the total tax take and to a basis on which this should be shared between the two counties which are parties to the agreement. The provisions of a double tax agreement which seek to reduce or eliminate double taxation are frequently described as affording treaty protection. There is some debate in a number of jurisdictions as to whether a double tax agreement can have the effect of imposing a liability to tax where none existed under domestic legislation or whether such an agreement is restricted in scope to providing relief from tax.

Double tax agreements serve to promote trade which in their absence would be discouraged by the prospect of double taxation. Apart from seeking to prevent double taxation, double tax agreements generally include provisions for the exchange of information between the two revenue authorities so as to prevent tax avoidance or evasion.

Unilateral relief

Although the principal purpose of a double tax agreement is to promote trade by giving investors the assurance that they will not be subject to double taxation, the tax legislation of the major capital exporting countries usually contains provisions which grant a measure of relief from double taxation even in the absence of a double tax agreement; so-called unilateral relief. The tax authorities in capital exporting countries recognise as a rule that they will not conclude double tax agreements with every potential capital importing country but nevertheless do not wish to discourage their residents from pursuing potentially attractive investment opportunities in a country with which no such agreement happens to have been concluded. It is for this reason that they have introduced provisions granting unilateral relief. However, such unilateral relief is likely to fall short of the relief afforded under the terms of a double tax agreement. It is often restricted to granting relief by way of deduction, instead of a credit, for overseas taxes suffered. If unilateral relief were as comprehensive as double tax relief, the capital importing country would have no incentive to conclude a double tax agreement with the capital exporting country. As a consequence, all the costs of eliminating double taxation would have to be borne by the exchequer of the capital exporting country.

Methods of granting relief from double taxation

As described previously, double taxation generally arises out of the competing claims of an investor's country of residence to tax his worldwide income and the country of source's assertion of its taxing rights over income arising within it. The principal means of overcoming the problem of double taxation involves the country of residence forgoing its taxing rights, either wholly or in part, in exchange for the country of source moderating its own claims. The country of source will often moderate its claims by delaying the point at which a resident of the other country becomes liable to tax in respect of business profits arising out of a trading activity undertaken within it and by reducing the rate of withholding tax applicable to dividends, royalties and interest payable to such residents.

The country of residence will adopt, as a rule, one of two bases on which to give its residents relief from double taxation; either the so-called exemption method or the credit method.

Exemption method

The exemption method involves the country of residence exempting from tax income with a foreign source. This represents an acceptance that the country of source should have the primary taxing rights in relation to income arising within it. However, certain countries which operate an exemption method will apply it only where a double tax agreement has been entered into with the country of source.

The exemption method avoids the distortions which arise under a credit method. These distortions arise where the host country raises its revenue through forms of taxation which are not comparable to the taxes levied in the home country and for which, as a consequence, no credit is available. They also arise where the host country offers tax incentives, either for specific industries or generally, because these tax incentives may be confiscated by the home country when the profits are remitted or deemed to have been remitted under a credit method.

A number of countries, most notably Germany, which in principle apply a system of worldwide taxation, grant exemption where a double tax agreement has been entered into in respect of the overseas income.

Credit method

So far as worldwide systems of taxation are concerned, these seek to overcome the problem of double taxation by granting their residents credit for the overseas taxes suffered. However, under such a system the investor will bear the higher of the tax liability in his home country or the liability in the host country. In the case of a shareholding in excess of a given percentage (usually 10 per cent), this credit relief will include not just withholding taxes, but also underlying overseas taxes borne by the profits out of which any dividend is distributed. The legislation in different countries will have its own conventions for determining which profits should be treated as having been distributed for the purpose of calculating the underlying rate of tax (eg last in first out, first in first out, or specified profits).

The precise mechanics for granting credit tend to vary from jurisdiction to jurisdiction. Apart from the computational complexities involved in these calculations, there are often circumstances when either no or insufficient relief is available for the overseas taxes actually suffered. For example, a UK parent company will not obtain relief for overseas taxes suffered in an accounting period when the subsidiary reports a loss (this could happen where the subsidiary incurs a significant non-deductible loss but otherwise generates taxable trading profits). Furthermore the UK, unlike some other countries, does not permit the aggregation of income from different investments so as to arrive at an aggregated figure for underlying taxes available for credit. Instead the credit available for overseas taxes has to be calculated on a source by source basis which is much more restrictive. In order to overcome this restriction, a number of UK-based multinationals route their overseas dividends through an offshore (often Dutch) intermediate holding company in order to average the underlying rates of tax. By using an offshore holding company, these multinationals convert overseas dividends from a variety of sources – with various underlying rates of tax attaching – into dividends from a single overseas source with averaged underlying rates of tax. This ensures that so far as possible effective relief is available for all overseas tax suffered, regardless of the fact that a proportion of this income may have come from a source with a higher rate of tax than the UK. (See Chapter 10: *Holding Companies and Co-ordination Centres* for a further description of this.)

Unlike the US and a number of other countries, the UK does not permit any excess foreign tax credits to be carried back against previous years' tax liabilities or carried forward to offset future liabilities.

Apart from the inevitable shortcomings involved in the calculation of the credit for overseas taxes, the system of worldwide taxation suffers from more fundamental defects of principle. In particular, a worldwide system does not give relief from double taxation where the taxes levied in the source country do not correspond to income, corporation or capital gains tax. This may be illustrated by using the example from Chapter 2: *Tax Systems and their Interaction*:

In example (a) Profits are subject to direct taxes at the rate of 50 per cent.

In example (b) No direct taxes are levied on business profits. Instead government revenue is raised by indirect taxes which increase costs by an amount equal to the direct taxes in (a).

	Example (a)	*Example (b)*
Turnover	1,000	1,000
Costs	800	900
Profit before tax	200	100
Less direct taxes 50%	100	–
Profit after tax	100	100

Assuming further that the profits are distributed in full to the parent company which is resident in a country which taxes the overseas dividend income of resident companies at a rate of 35 per cent, the calculations would be as follows:

		A		B
Dividends received (grossed up for underlying tax)		200		100
Corporation tax @ 35 per cent	70		35	
Less relief for underlying tax (100 restricted to 70)	70		–	
Additional tax liability in home country		–		35
Net cash available to investor (after tax in his home country)		100		65

In both cases, the actual net dividend received was £100. However, in example B, the investor incurs an additional tax liability of £35 in his home country, which reduces his after-tax dividend to £65 compared with the £100 in example A. This example illustrates the limitations of the worldwide system of taxation and emphasises the importance of evaluating any potential investment not just on the basis of the net of tax return in the host country but also after taking into account tax liabilities which may arise in the home country.

Where a host country offers tax incentives in order to encourage investment, these incentives will, as a rule, simply represent a tax deferral to an investor from a home country which taxes the worldwide profits of its residents. This is because the investor will be subject to tax in full when the profits are remitted to his home country by way of dividend or deemed dividend. Accordingly where such a system of taxation applies, the benefits of any tax incentives offered by a host country are taken away on remittance of the profits to the home country. In order to overcome this particular problem, a number of countries have included so-called tax-sparing provisions in their double tax agreements with certain developing countries.

Tax-sparing provisions

Tax-sparing involves the country of residence agreeing to 'honour' the tax incentives offered by the country of source. This is achieved by the country of residence deeming profits and income which benefit from a tax holiday to have been fully taxed in the country of source. This deemed tax is then available to offset any tax liability which would otherwise arise in respect of those same profits or income in the country of residence. The category of income and the type of incentive, to which any such tax-sparing provisions apply, are invariably narrowly defined in any double tax agreement containing such provisions.

Whereas the UK has entered into a large number of double tax agreements with such provisions, the US refuses as a matter of policy to agree to the inclusion of a tax-sparing provision in any double tax agreement which it negotiates.

Model agreements

It was agreed early in this century that the growth in international trade and the resulting problem of double taxation was an issue of international importance. In 1921, the League of Nations undertook the first of a series of studies of the issue. These studies culminated in the publication of a series of model double tax conventions. With the disbanding of the League of Nations, this work was taken up by the OECD's predecessor organisation and subsequently by the OECD which published a new Draft Double Tax Convention in 1963. This was followed by the extremely influential Model Double Tax Convention of 1977. The influence of the OECD Model Double Tax Convention lies in the fact that it provides a framework for negotiation, which already has the broad agreement of most developed countries. This both facilitated the negotiation of double tax agreements and exerted a harmonising influence over their structure and content.

So far as the development of these model agreements is concerned, the most significant feature is the increasing acceptance of the source country's taxing rights in relation to income arising within it. Originally, because the problem of double taxation had been an almost exclusive preoccupation of the major capital exporting countries, the solutions which they had proposed reflected a clear bias in favour of the country of residence.

In 1980, the UN issued a Model Double Taxation Convention between Developed and Developing Countries. Although this UN model adopts the same broad structure as the OECD model, it gives greater support to the taxing right of the country of source, ie the developing country. Thus a building site which lasts for more than six months will constitute a permanent establishment; this compares with the twelve-month period allowed by the OECD model. In addition, under the UN model, the provision of services, including consultancy services, for a period in excess of six months over a twelve-month period, will constitute a permanent establishment. Whereas the OECD Model Double Taxation Convention specifically excludes both "the maintenance of a stock of goods or merchandise . . . for the purpose of . . . delivery to customers" and "an independent agent acting in the ordinary course of his business" from the definition of a permanent establishment, the UN model treats the maintenance of stocks for delivery, even where these are held by an independent agent, as constituting a permanent establishment.

Principles underlying model conventions

A number of features of the OECD Model Double Taxation Convention of 1977 can be traced back to the earliest draft conventions drawn up by the Technical Committee of the League of Nations in the 1920s and 1930s. In particular, the OECD Convention adopts the same schedular approach as these earlier conventions, excluding from the definition of business income such specific items of income as dividends, royalties and interest.

Another fundamental feature of the OECD Model Convention, which was present in the earliest model agreements, is the arm's length principle. Because the price at which goods and services may be bought and sold within a group of companies would otherwise be open to manipulation in order to ensure that profits arose so far as possible in low tax jurisdictions, the arm's length principle enshrined in Article 9 (Associated Enterprises) permits tax authorities to adjust any artificial transfer price. Although the article does not go into detail as to the basis on which an arm's length price is to be determined, the Committee on Fiscal Affairs has produced two reports which address this issue: *Transfer Pricing and Multinational Enterprises* (1979) and *Transfer Pricing and Multinational Enterprises: Three Taxation Issues* (1984). The 1979 report recommended four methods for determining an arm's length price: the comparable uncontrolled price method, the resale price method, the cost-plus method and any other method which is acceptable. Although these same methods for determining the arm's length price were incorporated into the original regulations governing section 482 (Transfer Pricing) of the US Internal Revenue Code, the newly issued draft regulations appear to depart from this principle.

Where the revenue authorities in one country make a unilateral adjustment to intercompany charges, this will result in double taxation. To avoid this, it would be necessary for the revenue authorities in the other jurisdiction to permit a corresponding adjustment in the tax computation of the other associated company, which was a party to the transaction. Article 9(2) of the OECD Model Convention provides a basis for such an adjustment, when it states that the other state shall make an appropriate adjustment. However, this provision is inadequate because it does not compel the tax authorities in the second state to make the necessary adjustment. Even by invoking Article 25 – the so-called mutual agreement provision, which allows the taxpayer to refer a matter to the competent authorities where 'the actions of one or both of the contracting states result or will result for him in taxation not in accordance with the provisions of the Convention' – the taxpayer cannot be assured of a satisfactory outcome. This is because the competent authorities are not placed under any obligation either to reach agreement, or, failing that, to refer the matter to arbitration. The competent authority procedure is simply envisaged as a forum for discussion which may or may not reach a conclusion. It is in order to eliminate this central defect in the OECD Model Convention that the EC member states have agreed in principle to an Arbitration Convention (see Chapter 4).

Both Article 11, which deals with interest payments, and Article 12, which deals with royalty payments, contain provisions which restrict the right to a deduction where there is a special relationship between the payer and the recipient and the amounts are excessive. Although the UK revenue authorities have put forward the view that because the restriction in Article 11(6) applies by reference to the amounts of interest (and not just the rate), it has the effect of introducing a concept of thin capitalisation into the Model Convention or any agreement based on it, this view does not receive the support of the OECD which, in its report *Thin Capitalisation, Issues in International Taxation*, states that Article 11(6) prints the amount of interest to be corrected but not the recharacterisation of the relevant loan as a contribution to equity capital.

Article 7 (Business Profits), which lays down that a resident of one contracting state shall only become liable to tax in relation to business profits arising in the other contracting state when he sets up a permanent establishment in that other state, also lays down that the profits attributable to the permanent establishment should be determined on the basis that it is a distinct and separate enterprise, ie according to the arm's length principle. This involves separate accounting, with the branch preparing its accounts in accordance with this principle, as if it were an independent entity.

Although paragraph 4 of Article 7 permits the contracting state in which the permanent establishment is located to attribute profits to it on the basis of a formula apportionment, this is subject to the overriding requirement that the result should be in accordance with the principles contained in the Article. Although one commentator has expressed the view that this Article appears to run counter to the arm's length principle, it probably can be best understood as a pragmatic solution to the problem of determining profits in the absence of the necessary information. A number of countries have sought to overcome this problem in their domestic legislation by introducing a mandatory formula for attributing profits in such circumstances. Accordingly the provision simply legitimises the status quo, subject to the proviso that the result should equate to the profits as determined according to the arm's length principle.

Unitary tax (formula apportionment)

The application of the arm's length principle represents an attempt to arrive at the true economic profit arising in the various individual jurisdictions in which a company or group trades. On the other hand, unitary tax, which is sometimes referred to as a formula apportionment basis, simply applies a formula to solve the problem of determining how much of the profits of the whole should be attributed to the individual parts, ie the individual taxing jurisdictions. In the absence of international agreement as to both the formula to be applied and accounting standards, it is inevitable that double taxation will arise from such a basis of taxation. As a consequence, the widespread adoption of formula apportionment or the unitary basis of taxation would undermine the existing network of double tax agreements and necessitate their renegotiation on the basis of a commonly agreed formula. It would also involve the incorporation of formula apportionment into the domestic legislation of the countries concerned.

It is for this reason that there has been international concern at the adoption by California and a number of other states in the US of a unitary tax as a basis for levying state taxes. Apart from the profound objections of principle to which such a system of taxation gives rise, it imposes a considerable compliance burden on multinationals operating within the particular state as they are required to recompute their worldwide profits according to Californian (or the other states') accounting standards and to adjust these to take account of the tax regime. A legal challenge has been mounted on the question of the constitutionality of unitary tax. It is being argued that it interferes with the US Federal Government's exclusive authority in matters relating to the conduct of foreign affairs and the regulation of external trade. Although the litigation is being pursued by aggrieved taxpayers, it is supported by the US Federal Government which has filed an amicus curiae brief.

Bilateral or multilateral agreements

In an ideal negotiating situation, there should be a balance of investment between the countries which are parties to a double tax agreement. In addition, the two countries should have broadly similar tax systems and rates of tax. In these circumstances, the concessions granted under the terms of a double tax agreement would benefit the taxpayers or the fiscs of both countries equally.

In the case of a double tax agreement between a developed and a developing country, as the developing country is likely to have little or no outward investment, there will be a fundamental imbalance in the relationship between the two countries. In order to attract inward investment regardless of whether or not the investor's country of residence has entered into a double tax agreement, a developing country should adopt a tax system with this objective in mind and pitch its rate of tax accordingly. As a consequence, it will have little room for manoeuvre in any negotiations on a double tax agreement. Its principal concern will be to preserve its taxing rights in respect of income having a source within it as well as to preserve the benefit for overseas investors of any tax incentives which it may offer.

A capital exporting country will, as a rule, already provide some form of unilateral relief to its residents who invest overseas. As already mentioned, this is likely to fall short of the relief available under the terms of a double tax agreement. Accordingly, concluding a double tax agreement is likely to involve a cost to the exchequer of the capital exporting country. The granting of a tax-sparing provision would represent such a cost and one which is very open-ended, depending as it does on the extent to which the capital importing country is prepared to provide tax incentives. It is for this reason that the US will not agree to the inclusion of such a provision in any double tax agreement to which it is a party.

Because so many complex factors need to be taken into account in the negotiation of a double tax agreement, it is usual for these to be bilateral, ie, entered into by two countries, as opposed to multilateral in nature. Where multilateral conventions have been entered into, the countries concerned are generally at a similar stage of economic development and have similar tax systems. This was the case with the Comecon conventions, the Andean pact and the multilateral treaty signed by the Nordic countries. Apart from the need for a degree of economic convergence before such an agreement can be entered into, once in force it is cumbersome to amend or terminate.

Conflicts between tax systems

Because there are two incidences of tax under a classical system, one at the corporate level and the other at the shareholder level, this simplifies the process of negotiating double tax agreements. As previously stated, the negotiation of double tax agreements involves deciding on a basis on which the total tax take should be shared between the country of source and the country of residence. Under a classical system the tax imposed at the corporate level may be regarded as attributable to the source of the profits, whereas the tax imposed at the shareholder level can be taken to represent the tax on the return to the shareholder. Accordingly the tax on corporate profits should accrue to the source country, whereas the country of residence should have full taxing rights over the return to the shareholder. To achieve this, the country of source should waive all claims to withhold tax from dividend payments. Although the European Commission has been forced to allow certain member states to continue to apply withholding taxes to dividend payments for transitional periods, the parent/subsidiary directive reflects this same thinking. This is also the position which the Dutch adopt in the negotiation of double tax agreements.

However, under an imputation system this process is more complex. A tax system which integrates the liability of the company and the shareholder will inevitably impose a higher rate of tax in order to raise the same overall amount of revenue, than a tax system which imposes two separate incidences of tax. This was demonstrated when the UK increased its rate of corporation tax from 40 to 52 per cent on the introduction of its imputation system. (However, this principle has been obscured by the recent sharp reduction in the UK's rate of corporation tax, which coincided with a broadening of the tax base and a shift in the overall tax burden from direct to indirect taxes.) By integrating the liability of the shareholder and the company while at the same time increasing the rate of tax, it is less clear how much of the overall tax burden relates to the source of the profits and how much relates to the return to the shareholder. In the absence of withholding taxes on dividends under the majority of imputation systems, double tax agreements negotiated with such countries focus on obtaining a refund of a proportion of the underlying tax. The UK in its treaty network has been willing to concede the right to a refund of a proportion of this underlying tax to residents of the other country. However, this refund often does not flow directly to the overseas shareholder as it should do if it is indeed to put the overseas shareholder in a similar position to the UK resident shareholder. Instead the refund accrues in whole or in part to the other country's exchequer. This may be illustrated by an example of how the refund under the UK/Netherlands double tax agreement will affect a Dutch (indirect) shareholder.

Dutch company

Dividends received – exempt	1,000
Refund of proportion of ACT (Netherlands/UK DTA)	100
	1,100
Distribution to shareholders	1,100
Tax withheld – 35%	385
Received by shareholder	715

Thus the value of the refund to the overseas shareholder is reduced by the tax charge imposed by his country of residence. This reduction in the value of the refund accordingly represents a transfer of funds between the exchequers which partially undermines the attempt to overcome the problem of double taxation at the shareholder level.

Where income, taxed under an imputation system, flows to a company based in a country with a classical tax system which operates a system of worldwide taxation, the refund of ACT may simply represent a transfer between exchequers without benefiting the overseas shareholder at all.

Where, on the other hand, dividend income flows between companies in two imputation systems, it should be possible to ensure that tax suffered at the corporate level, in one country, is available as a credit to the shareholder in the other. The mechanism for achieving this would involve the tax legislation in the recipient country deeming the income from the overseas country to have a domestic source with an attaching tax credit. In order to compensate the exchequer of the recipient country for the cost involved in treating the income as tax paid and granting a tax credit, the revenue authorities in the country where the tax was actually paid would make a compensatory payment to the revenue authorities of the recipient country.

However, this solution has not been adopted under the double tax agreements, seeking to address this issue, which the UK has entered into. These provide for half of the tax credit to be refunded to an overseas corporate shareholder, subject to a deduction – from the dividend and the amount refunded – of a 5 per cent withholding tax. Accordingly, an overseas group can maximise the dividends which it takes from its UK group or subsidiary in order to maximise its refund of tax credit and so minimise the effective rate of tax which it suffers in respect of its UK activities. Depending on its tax profile in its home country, an overseas multinational can suffer a lower effective rate of tax than a UK-based company or group. The ability of overseas multinationals to maximise dividends (which simply represent internal transfers within a group) and in so doing to reduce their effective tax rate below that of a local competitor, accounts for the intransigence of the Germans to agree to a reduction in the rate of their withholding tax, when pressed in the negotiation of double tax agreements. However, this reduction in the effective rate of tax represents a deferral as the prejudice problem is likely to arise when ultimately the company distributes its overseas income to its shareholders and incurs a tax liability equivalent to the shareholders' tax credit.

Where dividend income flows from one country with an imputation system to an individual shareholder in another country (whether it operates an imputation system or not), a proportion of the tax credit should be made available to the overseas shareholder. This procedure is already adopted by the UK and a number of other countries operating an imputation system in their networks of double tax agreements. However, in order to ensure that the tax suffered at source is fully creditable in the shareholder's country of residence, the UK refunds the whole of the tax credit but applies a withholding tax to the 'gross' dividend. If, on the other hand, the shareholder were simply to suffer an element of irrecoverable tax credit, no relief is likely to be available for this as it will be regarded as underlying tax in the shareholder's country of residence.

Treaty shopping and anti-avoidance measures

Treaty shopping involves a resident of a country seeking to take advantage of a double tax agreement between countries outside his country of residence. He may wish to do this either because the country in which he is resident has not entered into a double tax agreement with the country in which he proposes to invest or alternatively because some other country has concluded a more favourable double tax agreement with the latter country.

The prevalence of treaty shopping has led to a significant growth in anti-avoidance measures, ranging from the use of domestic substance over form doctrines to the incorporation of specific anti-avoidance measures into the text of recent double tax agreements. Indeed the OECD Model Double Tax Convention includes in Articles 10, 11 and 12 the requirement that the recipient of dividends, interest or royalties should be the beneficial owner (as opposed to a mere intermediary) for the benefits of any treaty to apply. The US has taken this process further than most other countries by insisting on the inclusion of a so-called limitation of benefits clause in any new agreements which it concludes. This clause would limit the benefits of the agreement to true residents of the two countries (ie, excluding residents whose ownership was through a third country), thus reaffirming the bilateral nature of the agreement. In addition, US domestic law regards treaties as being on a par with federal law and, as a consequence, subsequently enacted federal law may override the provisions of a treaty. In the Technical and Miscellaneous Revenue Act 1988, the US has incorporated specific treaty override provisions into its domestic legislation. Such developments threaten to erode the value of treaty networks.

Conclusion

The growing popularity of imputation systems, the increasing frequency of the re-negotiation of double tax agreements as well as the uncertainty of interpretation which anti-abuse doctrines and treaty override provisions have introduced, threaten seriously to erode the value of treaties especially in relation to investment between developed countries. So far as investment in developing countries is concerned, the record of a number of these for adhering either to the letter or to the spirit of double tax agreements is at best undistinguished.

4
The Harmonisation of Direct Taxes in Europe

Because the right to levy taxes – and to decide on the form which these taxes should take – is fundamental to any nation's claim to sovereignty, it is not altogether surprising that only very limited progress has been made in harmonising direct taxes in Europe. Although greater progress has been made in harmonising indirect taxes, this is because the introduction of a value added tax (VAT) has from the start been regarded as a price of membership of the European Community. Indeed member states' contributions to the European Commission are based in part on the revenue which they raise from VAT.

So far as direct taxes are concerned, these taxes have evolved over long periods of time in response to the differing political systems and social objectives of individual member states. These member states have developed their own approach to the administration and enforcement of direct taxes and likewise their domestic populations have adopted their own attitude to the question of compliance. Because individual tax regimes are so deeply engrained, it is consequently unrealistic to expect speedy progress towards the harmonisation of direct taxes. The procedural requirement within the Community that tax measures may only be adopted by the unanimous vote of all member states has further guaranteed that progress will be slow.

The two illustrations below help to put the problems of tax harmonisation among the member states into a broader perspective. Figure 4.1, facing, shows the total tax revenue of each member state expressed as a percentage of gross domestic product. This ranges from 49.9 per cent in the case of Denmark to 33.2 per cent in the case of Greece.

Figure 4.2, facing, shows the differing extent to which the member states rely on the various forms of taxation to raise revenue.

Whereas Denmark raises 59.5 per cent of its total tax revenue through direct taxes on income and profits, France raises only 17.4 per cent from this source.

Why harmonise taxes?

In the absence of tax harmonisation, a company may be induced to locate production in a country (country A) with relatively high costs but a low

Figure 4.1 Total tax revenue as a percentage of GDP at market prices

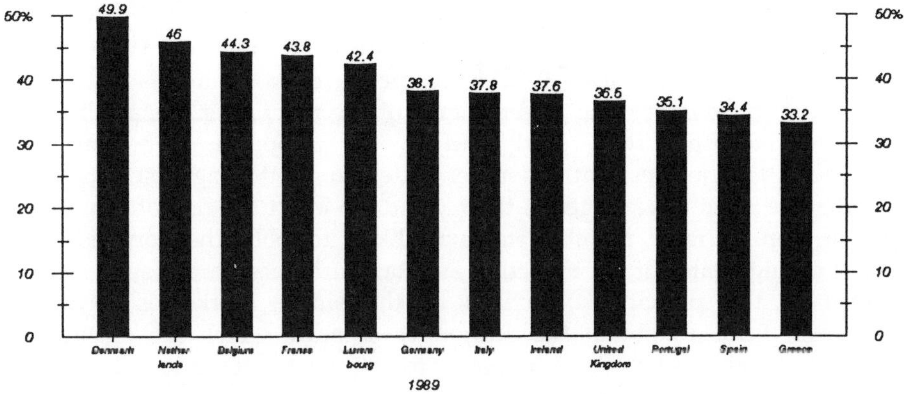

Countries have been ranked by their total tax to GDP rates

Source: OECD Revenue Statistics 1991 (see Appendix II)

Figure 4.2 Tax revenue of main headings as percentages of total tax revenue

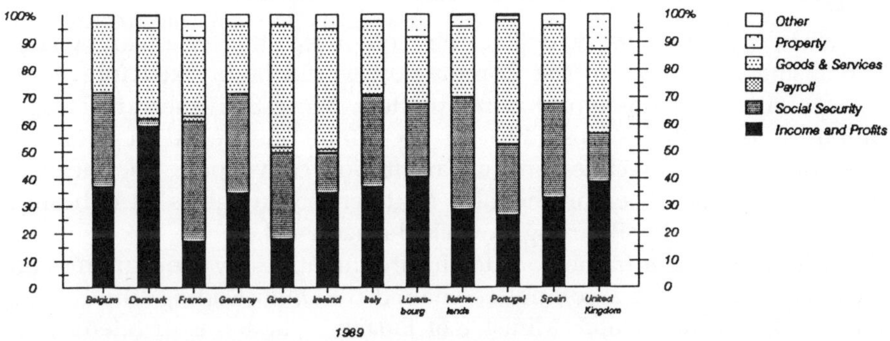

Source: OECD Revenue Statistics (see Appendix II)

rate of tax, rather than in a country (country B) with low costs but a higher rate of tax which results in a higher overall level of costs. This is because a company which centred its production in country A would be able to sell its products more cheaply, other things being equal, than a company which had located its production in country B. It is argued that this would lead to a misallocation of resources within the Community as production may gravitate towards countries with relatively high production costs but lower taxes.

Free-market economists, on the other hand, while accepting that tax considerations will affect the decision as to where to locate production, argue instead that tax is a cost just like any other cost of production and the fact that businesses will choose to locate in jurisdictions with the lowest overall costs will force the fiscs to moderate their demands. In the longer term, this will lead to a convergence of tax burdens within the Community. However, the governments of the member states are likely to be concerned that this could lead to the adoption of beggar your neighbour tax policies, with member states competing against each other to offer the most advantageous tax regime. To avert the risk of downward pressure on tax rates, member states are likely to lobby the Commission to maintain high rates of tax by acting as a tax gatherers' cartel.

One of the principal objectives of the single market is to enable European firms to obtain the economies of scale which are essential in today's global market-place in order to compete internationally. Indeed one of the principal aims of EC industrial policy is to foster this process by encouraging firms either to merge or to acquire companies across national borders and, in so doing, to create Pan-European companies to take advantage of the opportunities offered by the enlarged market. However, in the absence of tax harmonisation in Europe, tax obstacles would hinder the achievement of this objective.

Progress to date and the Ruding report

Just when practitioners had become convinced that the centralising, harmonising tendencies of the Commission would be blocked forever by the requirement for unanimity in tax matters, Mme. Scrivener, the current Commissioner with responsibility for tax affairs, succeeded in obtaining agreement to two directives and an arbitration convention. The fact that these proposals had been on the table for twenty years gives an indication of the extent of the breakthrough which she achieved.

In order to define a framework for future initiatives by the Commission, Mme. Scrivener set up a committee chaired by Onno Ruding (the Ruding committee), a former Dutch Minister of Finance. The terms of reference of this committee were to consider:

(1) whether differences in the tax regimes of member states were likely to result in distortions in the internal market, particularly in relation to investment decisions and competition;
(2) whether any such distortions would be eliminated by the interplay of market forces or whether action was required at the Community level;
(3) what specific measures, if any, would be required to remove distortions.

Although the Ruding committee has presented its report, only the conclusions have been published. Despite the Ruding committee's reluctance to recommend a particular tax system as the basis for harmonisation, in virtually every other respect the Ruding report represents a return to the original, ambitious conceptions of the Commission. The committee recommends a minimum and maximum rate of corporation tax of 30 and 40 per cent respectively, despite the incongruity of such a proposal in the absence of any recommendation as to the type of tax system to be adopted. The 40 per cent ceiling rate is recommended to be inclusive of any local taxes which, it is further recommended, should be calculated on the same basis as national corporation taxes.

The report also recommends that the tax base should be harmonised across member states. So far as existing or proposed directives are concerned, the thrust of the Ruding report is that they should go further and faster than originally envisaged. The principal recommendations in respect of these are included later in this chapter, in the section dealing with the directives and draft directives. The report defines a phased timescale for a wholesale harmonisation of tax regimes within the Community.

That the Ruding committee was sensitive to the fact that market forces could only result in downward convergence is apparent from the recommendation for a minimum rate of tax. Because the Ruding committee was alive to the possibility that interest or royalty income would be channelled out of the EC via a conduit jurisdiction without attracting any tax liability within the EC, it only recommended the abolition of withholding taxes subject to the proviso that the beneficiary should be taxed somewhere within the EC. Furthermore in order to counter the possibility of evasion, the Ruding committee recommended a uniform 30 per cent withholding tax on dividend distributions. However, this would be subject to waiver where the appropriate tax identification was produced.

A positive recommendation is that the Commission should work with member states to define a common treaty policy between member states as well as with third countries. This is particularly relevant to negotiations with the US as it is likely that member states will only be able to hold their own in such negotiations by combining forces.

Tax systems in the member states

The European Commission has not been able to agree on the type of tax system which should be used as a basis for harmonising tax systems within the Community. In 1963, the Neumark Committee suggested that the split-rate system should serve as the basis for harmonisation. However, in 1970 the Van den Tempel Report suggested that the classical system should be adopted as the model. In 1975, a draft directive on the harmonisation of systems of company taxation and withholding tax on dividends proposed the adoption of a partial imputation system as the basis for harmonisation. However, this draft directive was withdrawn and at present there are no proposals for the harmonisation of tax systems within the EC.

Only Luxembourg and the Netherlands have adopted classical tax systems under which profits accruing to companies are taxed twice: once at the corporate level and then on distribution, in the hands of shareholders. The other ten member states have integrated, to varying extents, the liability of companies and their shareholders. In the case of Greece, this integration is achieved by allowing companies a deduction in the computation of taxable profits for dividend distributions. In the case of France, Italy, Ireland and the UK, this integration is achieved by granting shareholders a full or partial credit for corporation taxes paid. Germany combines both these approaches by granting relief, in the form of a lower rate of tax, at the corporate level in respect of dividend distributions and by granting the shareholder full credit for taxes suffered at the corporate level. Belgium, Denmark, and Portugal provide relief from double taxation by subjecting dividend income to reduced rates of personal tax. (For full details of the tax systems operated by member states see Appendix I.)

Member states, which provide relief from double taxation when corporate profits are distributed to individual shareholders invariably only grant this relief in respect of their own taxes. In the case of imputation systems this issue is commonly referred to as the 'prejudice' problem. This arises when a company receives foreign source income which, because of the availability of double tax relief, is not subject to further tax in its hands, but for which, on distribution, the company must account nevertheless for advance corporation tax or the précompte or its equivalent. The Ruding report accepted that this 'prejudice' discriminated against cross border investment flows and would perpetuate the existing fragmentation of capital markets within the Community. Accordingly, it recommended that a member state whose tax system provides relief from double taxation in respect of domestically earned corporate profits on their distribution to shareholders, should be required to extend this relief to include corporate profits which are earned in other member states. The Ruding report recommended that this extension of the relief should apply to both imputation and other systems for providing relief from double taxation.

However, the fragmentation of capital markets is likely to persist so long as the tax credit available to domestic shareholders under imputation systems is not available equally to shareholders based in other member states. The Ruding report specifically did not recommend that these tax credits should be extended to non-resident shareholders even though some member states already provide, under the terms of bi-lateral double tax agreements, for such an extension. The justification for the Ruding committee's failure to advocate the extension of the tax credit in this way was that it would conflict with the principle of source country entitlement. This is surprising as the willingness of certain member states to concede, under the terms of a double tax agreement, part or the whole of the tax credit to shareholders in another member state would appear to represent an acceptance that the integration of the corporate tax liability and the personal tax liability of the shareholder had resulted in a higher rate of tax than would otherwise have been the case and that this exceeded their entitlement under the source country principle.

Rates of tax and tax bases

In making an investment decision, an investor will be concerned to know the marginal rate of tax, ie the rate of tax which each additional pound or dollar of profits will attract. Where, however, he is reviewing the overall performance of either a group, company or division, he will be concerned to know the average rate of tax, ie the total tax charge expressed as a percentage of total profits.

The calculation of any actual or potential tax liability is a function of both the nominal rate of tax and the tax base, ie the adjusted profits for tax purposes. To illustrate how misleading it can be to consider only one element of this calculation in isolation, the UK had a high nominal rate of tax before 1984 (52 per cent) which because of generous tax allowances for investment in stocks (inventory) and plant and machinery resulted in a low effective rate of tax. Although the nominal rate of tax has been reduced to 33 per cent, for a large number of businesses the effective rate of tax is now much higher than it was before 1984 because the allowances for investment in stocks were withdrawn, and those for plant and machinery substantially reduced, at the same time as the nominal rate of tax was reduced.

To harmonise tax regimes it would be necessary to harmonise not only tax systems but also bases and rates of tax. However, because the harmonisation of tax systems presents intractable political problems, the Commission, in 1988, limited its objectives to the harmonisation of the tax base and issued a preliminary draft proposal on this subject. The intention behind this proposal was to ease the way for small and medium-sized enterprises to do business in other member states. At present, the significant differences between the tax regimes of the various member states mean that it is difficult for enterprises to engage in business in another member state without first incurring, often considerable, professional fees in order to identify the pitfalls that are a consequence of these differences.

Turning to the draft directive itself, this was intended to apply to all types of undertaking. The draft directive set out to define, in the most general of terms, guidelines for a basis of valuing assets and for calculating provisions as well as a framework for the tax deductibility of expenses. The draft directive defined the taxes to which it would apply as the member states' equivalents of income, corporation and capital gains tax.

Capital gains

The draft specifically stated that capital gains should be included in the tax base. Capital losses would equally have been deductible. There was a provision which would have allowed any liability in respect of a capital gain to be deferred where the taxpayer reinvested, within a specified time, the proceeds of the disposal which gave rise to the gain. The draft directive permitted member states to treat the transfer of an asset between member states as taking place at market value and as crystallising a capital gain, although provisions were included to avoid the possibility of double taxation arising.

Depreciation

The definition of depreciable assets was linked to the 4th Directive on company accounts. It included buildings, plant and machinery, patents and similar intangible property. In keeping with practice on the continent, the draft directive clearly intended that tax depreciation should be aligned with the depreciation charge in the commercial accounts.

So far as fixed assets were concerned, depreciation would have applied for the period in which the asset was acquired or produced. This charge would have been based on the purchase price, inclusive of incidental costs and irrecoverable value added tax, or on the cost of production and would have been net of any subsidy received. An enterprise would have had the option to calculate depreciation either on a straight-line basis or on the reducing balance method. This latter method would have been subject to overall limits as to both the applicable percentage rate and the level of charge. Although the choice of the straight-line method would have been irrevocable, the choice of the reducing balancing method could have been revoked. In the case of intangible assets, the straight-line method would have been mandatory. Certain incidental categories of fixed asset could have been included at a base stock valuation, ie at a fixed amount on the basis that neither quantity nor value would vary significantly. Other low value items may have been deducted in full from taxable profits in the period of acquisition.

Where the applied depreciation charge proved to be out of line with actual experience, exceptional depreciation could have been charged.

Other rules defined the basis on which formation expenses, expenses in connection with the creation of trade marks or names, should be written off. Research and development expenditure could have been written off either as incurred or over a five-year period.

Provisions

Apart from provisions for ordinary accruals, provisions would have been permitted only in respect of losses or charges which were either certain or likely to be incurred, but where there was uncertainty as to the amount. Where a provision was no longer required, the proposed directive required it to be reincorporated in the profits.

Stocks

Stocks (inventories), which were defined as raw materials and consumables, work in progress, and finished goods and goods for resale, were to be valued at their purchase price or production cost. Certain stocks, of which neither the quantity nor value varied significantly, could be valued according to the base stock method. Otherwise, where the purchase price or production cost of goods could not be readily ascertained, such stocks could be valued on the basis of a weighted average price or on the basis of the FIFO (first in, first out) or LIFO (last in, first out) method.

Where there was a reduction in value of an item of stock, it could be written down. The value of the item could be revalued (upwards), if its value subsequently increased. However, any revaluation could not exceed the purchase price or cost of production.

The proposal provided that a capital gain may have been recognised when stocks were transferred either to or from permanent establishments in different member states, although the gain would have been deferred until it was effectively realised. The item would have been reflected in the accounts in the member state to which it was transferred at market value, except where it is transferred to the 'home' member state in which case it could have retained its original value subject to the proviso that steps would have to be taken to avoid double taxation.

Expenses and other charges

Penalties and fines were specifically disallowed. However, the decision as to whether, or to what extent, voluntary payments should be deductible would have been left to member states. Otherwise expenditure would have been deductible to the extent that it contributed to the production of taxable income.

Other assets (either fixed or current)

The proposal provided that these should be valued at purchase price or production cost. Provisions were permitted to take account of any diminution in the value of these assets. Such a provision may have been by way of percentage deduction, based on experience. Where the value of an asset subsequently increased, the provision would have been reversed.

Final provisions

The proposal stated explicitly that it would not preclude national measures to prevent fraud and evasion. It specifically enjoined member states to ensure that no unjustified tax advantages were obtained by virtue of the proposal. The proposal further recommended the establishment of an advisory committee to oversee the harmonisation process.

The Ruding committee endorsed the need for harmonisation of the tax base and recommended the setting up of a study group to consider this issue further. The Ruding committee highlighted the need to harmonise the following, additional specific areas: leasing, occupational pensions, pension contributions for expatriate workers, headquarter costs, thin capitalisation. Although not ruling out the use of tax incentives as an instrument of economic policy, the Ruding committee recommended that such incentives should not be incorporated in the tax base. However, the conclusions of the Ruding report do not address the issue of the deductibility of interest incurred in financing investment in other member states. This represents a major omission.

The package of three measures and existing draft directives

This section considers in greater detail the package of three measures which were adopted in July 1990 as well as the draft directives which are currently on the table. It also considers the possible implications of the Ruding report on these various measures.

Mergers and reorganisations

The tax systems of the larger member states contain provisions aimed at eliminating, or at least reducing, at a national level the tax obstacles to the restructuring of industry. These provisions rarely, if at all, enable this restructuring to occur across borders, between member states. In the words of the so-called convergence report from the Commission to the Council it is extremely important that firms should be of a size to handle the technical and economic conditions characterising the modern production apparatus, to exploit the scope for large-scale production afforded by the establishment of the common market and to meet the requirements of increasing competition both within the Community and in the world at large. In order to facilitate the restructuring necessary to achieve this, a directive was adopted on mergers, divisions and contributions of assets taking place between corporations of different member states. This directive provides for capital gains arising from a merger, division or contribution of assets, or an exchange of shares, not to be taxed when the transaction is effected but only when the gain is actually realised.

Although this directive represents a step in the right direction, it stops short of addressing the structural problems arising out of differences in the tax systems of member states. The directive also fails to deal with the question of stamp duties and transfer taxes which often constitute a sizeable, albeit one-off, cost associated with corporate reorganisations.

Another criticism which has been levelled at this directive is that it tries to deal with a number of tax issues associated with European mergers and reorganisations before the fundamental issues of company law have been resolved. For example, certain member states (including the UK) do not have company law provisions which would permit the fusion or merger (as opposed to an acquisition) between domestic and other EC companies. Furthermore, the application of the directive is limited to capital companies. For these reasons, a number of impediments will remain in the way of European mergers.

Parent/Subsidiary Directive – dividends

The Council Directive *On the Common System of Taxation Applicable in the case of parent companies and subsidiaries of different Member States* was the second measure concluded in July 1990. This directive aims to:

(1) eliminate withholding taxes on dividend payments by subsidiaries to their parent companies where these are based in the EC;
(2) ensure that tax relief is available at the parent company level for taxes suffered in respect of dividends from subsidiaries.

For the purposes of the directive, a parent company is defined as a company in a member state which has a 25 per cent holding in the capital of a company (the subsidiary) in another member state.

Withholding taxes

The directive exempts from withholding tax dividends received by a parent company in one member state from a subsidiary in another member state. There is a requirement that any shareholding must have been held for an uninterrupted period of two years for the directive to apply. However, the directive allows withholding taxes to continue to apply to the payment of dividends by subsidiaries based in Germany, Portugal and Greece. In the case of Germany and Portugal such withholding taxes may be retained only until 31 December 1996 and 31 December 1999 respectively. Because of the special characteristics of its tax system, Greece may retain withholding taxes on the payment of dividends for so long as the structure of its tax system remains unchanged.

The directive does not apply to the advance corporation tax which is a feature of both the UK and Ireland's imputation systems, nor does it apply to the French précompte, as these are not withholding taxes.

Tax relief for dividends
The directive further requires the member state in which the parent company is resident to grant relief from tax for dividends received from a subsidiary based in another member state. This relief may be by way of:

(1) exemption from tax; or
(2) foreign tax credit for both the appropriate proportion of corporation tax in respect of the distributed profits and any withholding tax, where applicable.

The directive permits the member state in which the parent company is resident to deny, in the computation of taxable profits, the deduction of those costs which relate to the holding of the investment in the subsidiary. Where member states (such as France) quantify this disallowance by deeming a certain percentage of the costs to relate to any such shareholding, this percentage may not exceed 5 per cent of the distributed profits.

Because this directive applies only to capital companies, the Ruding report recommends that its scope should be extended to include all forms of business enterprise. In addition, the Ruding report recommends that the directive should apply to shareholdings significantly below the current 25 per cent threshold.

Arbitration convention

The third measure agreed by the Council of Ministers in July 1990 was the so-called arbitration convention. Because this measure is in the form of a convention, it requires ratification by all member states before it comes into effect.

The convention seeks to overcome the problem of double taxation which would otherwise arise where one member state unilaterally adjusts (for its own tax purposes) the prices at which transactions have taken place between associated companies within the Community. It does this by requiring that a corresponding adjustment shall be made in the other member state and by defining a procedure for consultation between the relevant authorities of the member states concerned. In the absence of agreement, the convention establishes an arbitration procedure presided over by an advisory commission which includes representatives of the member states concerned as well as representatives of other member states. This advisory commission can make a binding decision as to the appropriate corresponding adjustment. In this respect, the arbitration convention goes beyond the so-called mutual agreement procedure contained in most double tax agreements, which does not compel the parties to agree on the appropriate adjustment.

Apart from recommending the early ratification of the convention, the Ruding report recommends that the Commission should take action, together with member states, to establish rules and procedures governing transfer pricing adjustments between member states.

Draft directives

Parent/subsidiary – royalty and interest payments

A draft directive was issued on 24 January 1991 which proposed that interest or royalties paid by a subsidiary to its parent company should be exempt from withholding tax. This draft directive adopts the same definition of a parent/subsidiary relationship as the directive on dividend payments between subsidiaries and their parents, ie the parent company must own at least 25 per cent of the capital of the subsidiary.

This draft directive contained a fundamental defect in that it would have eliminated withholding taxes only on payments between parent companies and their subsidiaries. As it is more usual for such payments to flow between subsidiary companies, especially where a group finance or licensing company is involved, withholding taxes would have continued to apply in such cases. The European Parliament has proposed an amendment which extends the application of the draft directive to cover interest and royalties paid by any enterprise in one member state to any enterprise in another member state. This amendment, which goes beyond correcting the defect referred to above, has been adopted in a revised draft.

Because the complete abolition of withholding taxes would have presented Greece and Portugal with budgetary problems, the draft directive proposes to allow these member states a transitional period of seven years. For the first five years, they would be allowed to continue to levy withholding taxes but at a rate which could not exceed 10 per cent; for the two final years this rate would be reduced to 5 per cent. The Council of Ministers would have discretion to extend this transitional period should this be necessary.

The Ruding report called for the complete abolition of withholding taxes on interest and royalty payments between enterprises within the Community. However, the report also proposed that accompanying measures should be introduced to ensure that the income is taxed within the Community in the hands of the beneficiary.

Losses of permanent establishments and subsidiaries situated in other member states

The draft directive on 'the taking into account by enterprises of the losses of their permanent establishments and subsidiaries' represents one of the most radical proposals to emanate from the Commission. The starting point for the proposal is that there is no justification for discriminating against the form of enterprise, whether a branch or subsidiary. The choice between the two should be a purely commercial matter, unaffected by tax considerations.

The other underlying principle is that relief should be available in the 'home' member state for losses incurred in another member state. Accordingly this relief should be available regardless of whether the loss was incurred through a branch or subsidiary.

Although a worldwide system of taxation will generally grant relief in the home country for the losses of an overseas branch and, by the same token, levy tax on any profits arising from it, the granting of relief for the losses of an overseas branch conflicts with the fundamental logic of an exemption method. However, certain countries with an exemption method have introduced specific provisions to grant such a relief while providing for the automatic recapture (reintegration) of any deduction so allowed, after a defined period. In the absence of a provision for the recapture of the deduction, instead of representing a tax deferral it would represent a permanent tax saving because future profits of the branch would not be taxed by virtue of the exemption. But, if the losses of the branch could not be carried forward and as a consequence future profits of the branch were taxed in the host country, the provision in the home country for the recapture of the previous deduction would give rise to double taxation. The Commission in this draft directive has provided that member states which apply an exemption system should allow relief for the losses incurred by branches in other member states, while at the same time providing for the automatic recapture of any deduction so granted, after six years. In order to overcome the potential problem of double taxation, the Commission has emphasised that this proposal should be adopted in conjunction with a proposal for the carry-over of company losses which was first put forward in 1984.

The other radical aspect of this draft directive is that it provides for relief to be available in the 'home' member state for the losses of a subsidiary based in another member state. Accordingly the losses of both branches and subsidiaries would be eligible for relief. In the case of a subsidiary, this loss would be computed by reference the tax laws of the member state in which the subsidiary was based. This feature of the draft directive is thought to have given rise to hostile initial responses from the revenue authorities of the various member states.

In addition to recommending the adoption of the draft directive on losses of permanent establishments and subsidiaries, the Ruding report recommends the phased introduction of full vertical and horizontal offsetting of losses within groups of enterprises at the national level. This would be a prelude to the introduction of full Community-wide loss offsetting within groups of enterprises. However, apart from being difficult to police, such Community-wide loss offsetting would exert inevitable downward pressure on the tax rates of those member states which had maintained relatively high rates of tax. For this reason, it is likely that this proposal will be strongly resisted.

Other non-tax measures

In order to facilitate the process of the economic integration of the Single Market, the European Commission has developed one distinctive Pan-European entity, the European Economic Interest Grouping, and is in the process of developing another, the European company. Tax practitioners need to be aware, in general terms, of the nature of these entities and of the tax issues involved in their use.

European Economic Interest Grouping

The European Economic Interest Grouping (EEIG) was created by a regulation which took effect on 1 July 1989. The regulation sets out the principal characteristics of the EEIG, while leaving certain issues to be clarified in the national implementing legislation. The most fundamental of these issues is the question of whether it has a separate legal personality. Under the UK implementing legislation, an EEIG does have a separate legal personality.

What is an EEIG?

An EEIG is formed by way of a contract between members. This contract supplements the rules contained in the regulation itself, which set out the basis for its governance and define the relationship between the members. The membership of an EEIG must comprise at least two companies or two natural persons, or combination thereof, based in different member states.

The contract, apart from containing details of voting rights, profit and loss allocations and management, must contain the EEIG's name, its objects, details of members, duration and official address. The official address of an EEIG is of particular importance as this determines the member state whose national laws will govern the contract.

The European company statute

The European Commission has issued a draft regulation, setting out the framework for a specifically European company. Unlike German, French, Dutch or any other type of company which is clearly identified with the member state of its original incorporation, the European company, being a creature of European law, is intended to transcend individual member states. In this respect, it would appear to represent an ideal vehicle for undertaking a business activity which extends to a number of member states within the Single Market. Indeed the Commission envisages the use of the 'mergers' directive as the principal means of forming a European company out of established businesses. The mergers directive would enable this restructuring to take place without giving rise to a tax liability in respect of any capital gains until such a time as the gains were actually realised.

Although the European company would be a creature of European law, under the proposals, the law of the member state in which it has its registered office would determine the structure of the board of directors, ie, whether there is a supervisory board along continental lines, as well as a board of executive directors. National law would also define the responsibility and authority of the board(s) of directors.

In order to promote the use of the European company as a Pan-European vehicle for undertaking business activities within the Single Market, the regulation originally included a provision which would have permitted the fiscal consolidation of the results of a European company's permanent establishments along the lines set out in the draft directive on losses of permanent establishments. However, the Commission has recently dropped this feature from the proposal.

The regulation on the European company is supplemented by a proposed directive defining a basis for employee participation which goes beyond the existing practices of a number of member states. This feature of the European company, combined with restrictions on the ownership of such an entity, is thought likely to limit its appeal. The restrictions on ownership prevent residents of non-member states from owning a European company.

Conclusion

The decision of the Commission to turn its back on its original ambitions, such as the harmonisation of tax systems and bases, in favour of the more pragmatic goal of eliminating distortions within existing systems, was rewarded by the adoption of the two directives and the arbitration convention. This progress was especially gratifying as these proposals had been on the table for a number of years. It remains to be seen whether this momentum can be maintained by the adoption of the proposed directives on losses and interest and royalty payments.

The Ruding report represents a return to the original, all-embracing ambitions of the Commission and as such is likely to have very little influence. This is especially so as it failed to address directly the biggest single obstacle to the integration of European capital markets, namely the disparity between tax systems. The most pressing aspect of this problem is the need for the tax credit available to domestic shareholders under imputation systems to be made equally available to shareholders in other member states. It may be necessary to introduce a clearing-house mechanism in order to achieve this. However, in the absence of some measure of harmonisation, groups which merge across member states will be forced to adopt contrived structures, such as the stapled stock structures described in Chapter 5, in order to try to overcome this particular obstacle.

5

Stapled Stocks, Income or Dividend Access Schemes, and Hybrid Structures

Introduction

Traditionally companies did not tax plan with a view to maximising net of tax returns to shareholders or particular groups of shareholders. This approach was often perfectly justifiable when the majority of shareholders and the multinational were resident in the same jurisdiction. However, with the internationalisation of security markets, the shareholder profile of the larger multinationals is tending to become more international. This is particularly so in smaller economies where the larger companies are forced to look overseas for investment opportunities and in turn attract a following among international investors who are themselves looking for value beyond their national frontiers. It is significant that considerable interest in stapled stock, income or dividend access schemes, and other hybrid structures has been generated in Australia, where the internationalisation of the stock market in the 1980s and the search of Australian-based multinationals for growth in overseas markets made it essential to seek to maximise returns to overseas shareholders.

The problem of the inherent incompatibility of different types of tax system was accentuated by the adoption in the 1970s and 1980s of imputation systems by an increasing number of developed countries. These arguably discriminate against overseas investors to the extent that the tax credit available to domestic shareholders is not granted directly to an ultimate, overseas shareholder (see Chapter 2, page 26). The internationalisation of shareholder profiles meant that it became increasingly common for shareholders to own shares in an overseas company which derived significant amounts of income from their country of residence. Where their country of residence operated an imputation system, such a structure often had the perverse effect of simply depriving such shareholders of the tax credit to which they would have been entitled if their dividend income had flowed directly from a company which shared their tax residence. This meant that it became essential to take into account the tax treatment of dividends in the hands of overseas shareholders in any exercise in international tax planning. This can be illustrated as shown in Figure 5.1:

Figure 5.1

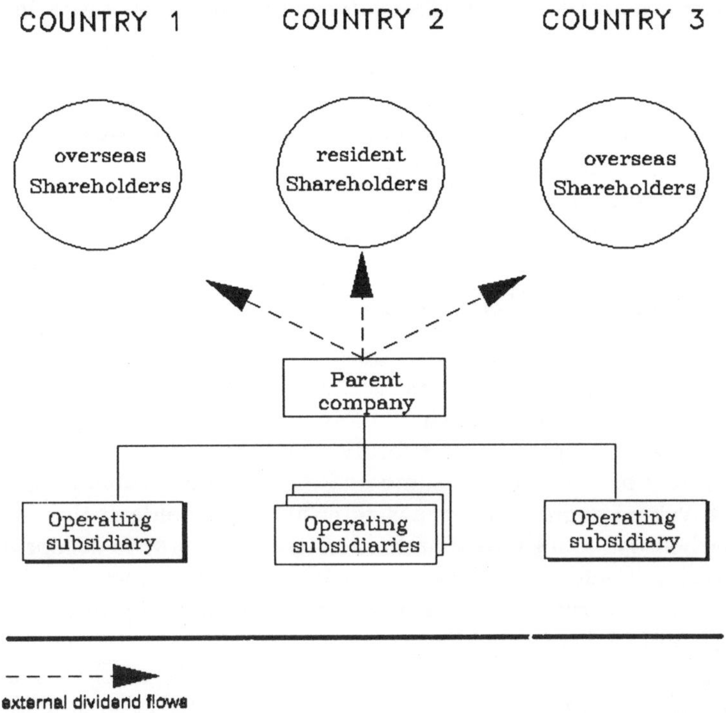

This mismatch of the shareholder/corporate structure was most likely to occur where an acquisition or takeover was undertaken in a foreign country, especially if the acquisition or takeover was by way of a share-for-share offer or involved raising capital in the domestic market of the target company.

Not only do imputation systems discriminate against overseas shareholders, but arguably they also discriminate against overseas income (the so-called 'prejudice' problem, see Chapter 2 *Tax Systems and Their Interaction*). Where companies have sufficient domestic income out of which to finance their dividend payments, this 'prejudice' may not be apparent. However, where such companies have to meet their dividend requirements out of overseas income, the majority of imputation systems have a mechanism similar to the UK's advance corporation tax or the French 'précompte', which acts, in all but name, as a withholding tax to ensure that sufficient domestic tax is accounted for at the corporate level in order to satisfy the tax credit granted to shareholders.

The advent of the single market in Europe is likely to bring these problems to the fore, as residents of member states invest increasingly across national borders. Although the corporate sector's 'domestic' market will grow from an economic perspective, the tax legislation of the various member states is likely to continue to remain rooted in the individual member states and this will affect adversely companies based in member states with imputation systems. This will be especially serious for companies based in member states with relatively small domestic economies, in relation to the rest of the single market, and with high levels of outward investment both in other member states and outside the single market. In the absence of harmonisation, a number of multinational companies will be forced to adopt innovative alternatives to conventional structures in order to overcome these problems.

A conventional structure

Before trying to define a stapled stock company, an income or dividend access scheme, and a hybrid structure, it is useful to define a conventional structure for a multinational. This involves a parent company based in one jurisdiction with a number of subsidiaries or associated companies some of which may be based in the same jurisdiction whilst others will be based overseas. Where such a group has minority shareholders, this is likely to be either because a body of shareholders was reluctant to accept the terms of an otherwise successful takeover or because the domestic legislation of the country concerned requires a degree of local participation, eg India, Indonesia and Malaysia.

What are stapled stock companies, income or dividend access schemes, and hybrid structures?

Stapled stocks

A stapled stock consists of shares in two separate entities based in different jurisdictions which are traded together. The precise mechanics for ensuring that the shares in the two entities cannot be traded separately will depend on the legal systems of the countries in which these entities are based.

In addition, there will often be an overlapping of management structure between the two entities which will serve to reinforce the ties between them. Thus although the two entities will constitute a group in a wider economic sense, the shareholders will receive dividends from two separate sources.

Income or dividend access schemes

Income or dividend access schemes involve shareholders being granted an entitlement to receive their dividend income, directly or indirectly, from a subsidiary company. It is usual for this entitlement to be met out of the profits of a company which is resident in the same country as the shareholder. Depending on the precise arrangements adopted, the income access shares may be issued to shareholders and may or may not be stapled to the shares of the ultimate parent company. Under other arrangements, the shareholder will not receive separate shares but may elect to receive a dividend from the income of a subsidiary, while at the same time, waiving his dividend entitlement from the parent company. This latter arrangement is usual where the income access shares are owned by a trust of which the resident shareholders, who have made the necessary election, are the beneficiaries.

Hybrid structures

For the purpose of this chapter any structure which cannot be described as a stapled stock or income or dividend access scheme and yet seeks to segregate the interests of an economic group into parallel companies based in different jurisdictions has been described as a hybrid structure. The presence of minority shareholders in such a structure will reflect essentially financial considerations as opposed to being an historical accident or simply reflecting compliance with a regulatory requirement.

The commercial reasons for adopting an unconventional structure

Apart from tax reasons, there are a number of commercial reasons why it may be appropriate to adopt such a structure. These are principally:

(1) the desire to reduce a group's exposure to political risk. Indeed the fear of an impending war in Europe and the desire to put overseas assets out of the reach of an invading power was the original reason for the Nestlé group adopting a stapled stock structure in the 1930s;
(2) the desire to place part of a group's assets outside the framework of an unduly onerous regulatory environment, eg the USA, which prohibits the payment of certain commissions or compliance with other jurisdictions' boycott restrictions;
(3) the desire or need to develop a profile in an overseas market. For example, this may be essential if it is intended to compete for defence contracts;
(4) the ability to tap a number of sources of finance.

Tax considerations involved in stapled stocks, income or dividend access schemes and hybrid structures

The primary objective of such structures is avoid the multiplication of tax liabilities which inevitably arises when income is routed through a number of jurisdictions. In the case of a multinational with overseas shareholders, income will pass through a number of jurisdictions: specifically the country of source of the profits, any intermediate jurisdiction(s) and the country of residence of the parent company, before finally passing by way of dividend into the hands of the shareholder in his country of residence. The greater the number of jurisdictions through which income passes, the greater will be the erosion which the income will suffer through taxation. This problem will be made worse where there is a structural incompatibility between the tax systems through which the income passes.

Stapled stocks, income or dividend access schemes, and hybrid structures are a means of giving overseas shareholders direct access to income arising from a subsidiary based outside the country of residence of the parent company. This is especially relevant where the income arises in the overseas shareholders' country of residence and has a tax credit attaching to it which can be preserved for their benefit. In addition, such structures are relevant where they enable overseas income to:

(1) by-pass the country of residence of the parent company and flow directly into the hands of overseas resident shareholders (who are also resident outside the country of source of the profits);

(2) flow directly into the hands of resident shareholders, thus avoiding the double taxation of corporate profits which arises under a classical system. This would be particularly relevant where the country of residence of the parent company applied a system of worldwide taxation and the overseas income had suffered little or no direct tax in the country of source.

This can be best illustrated by adapting the diagram in Figure 5.1 to show the revised income flows (see Fig 5.2 opposite).

In setting up any such structure, it is clearly necessary to ensure that both the country of source of the profits and the country of residence of the parent accept the validity of the mechanism for both segregating the income and directing it into shareholders' hands, so that any tax credit is preserved in the country of source and corporate or withholding taxes are avoided in the country of residence. In particular, it is important to ensure that any controlled foreign company type legislation does not deem any low-taxed, overseas income to be income of the parent.

Where an existing, conventional structure is being adapted to offer shareholders an option to receive dividend income directly from an overseas source, it is essential to ensure that the process of diverting this income is not treated as giving rise to a disposal for capital gains tax, or as a distribution for income tax, purposes. Where the structure is being put in place at the time of a takeover or merger, this may offer a certain

Figure 5.2

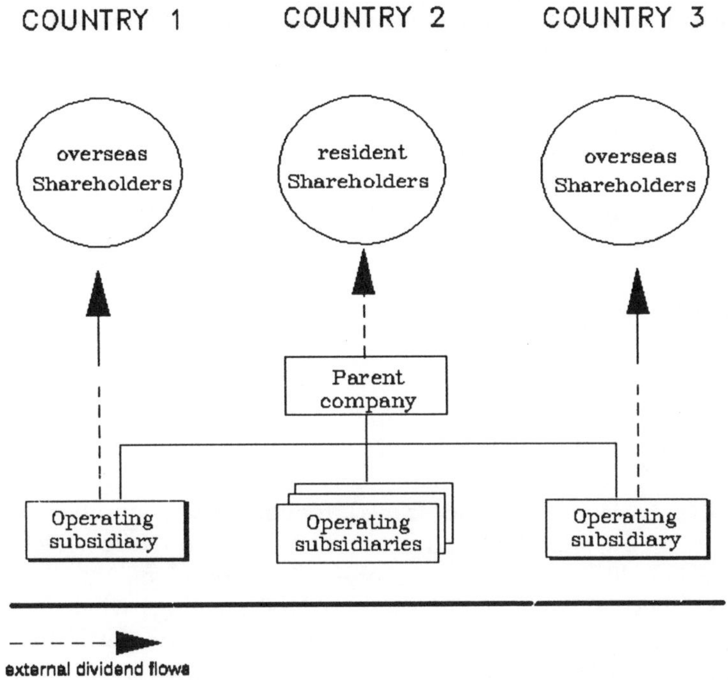

flexibility as the terms of the takeover or merger may be defined at the outset, specifically to avoid any such risk. A merger or agreed takeover will offer greater flexibility than would be the case with a contested takeover as the parties will have the opportunity to reorganise the share capital prior to the actual merger in order to avoid the pitfalls which a subsequent reorganisation of the share capital may entail.

Where such structures are used in a merger or takeover, they may enable existing shareholders to exchange their shares for shares in another company and in this way to defer any capital gains tax liability which would have arisen in the event of an all cash offer.

Certain countries apply restrictions on, or penalties to, the ownership of foreign property by certain categories of tax privileged organisation, such as pension or retirement saving schemes. Accordingly, if income access shares can be so structured that they are accepted as domestic property in the country from which the income flows, the overall market for the shares may be expanded and the share price enhanced as a consequence.

A number of countries have anti-avoidance legislation which is specifically targeted at this type of structure. In particular the US Internal Revenue Code of 1986 contains Section 269B, which is complex in its application and draconian in scope. Australia recently introduced anti-avoidance legislation designed to limit the attractions of such structures. Although there were suggestions that the original legislation had not been satisfactorily drafted to achieve its desired effect, it is difficult to understand why the commentators thought that the Australian revenue authorities would not take the trouble to amend the legislation bearing in mind that the investing public has to be informed of the tax attractions of a complicated structure.

Where the tax legislation provides a formal advance clearance procedure which operates satisfactorily in practice, it would clearly be desirable to ensure that any proposed structure will achieve its desired effect by obtaining such a clearance.

Examples of stapled stocks

Nestlé

The classic and best known example of a stapled stock structure was the Nestlé group. This consisted of shares in Nestlé SA, a Swiss corporation, and Unilac Inc., a Panamanian corporation. The shares of these two companies were quoted and traded together on a number of overseas stock markets. Unilac Inc. had a two-tier share structure which consisted of founders' shares and bearer shares. Only founders' shares carried the right to attend and vote at the shareholders' meetings which were held in Panama; these shares were all owned beneficially by Nestlé SA and were held in trust. The bearer shares in Unilac Inc. contained the stipulation that the bearer was only entitled to the benefits arising to shareholders provided he also held a share of Nestlé SA with the same serial number.

Through its ownership of the founders' shares and by its representation on the board of Unilac Inc., Nestlé maintained effective control of Unilac and provided unity and cohesion of management to the combined group. Commercial and tax considerations determined which entity should own (directly or indirectly) a particular subsidiary.

The shares in Nestlé SA contained no requirement that the shareholder should also be entitled to a corresponding share in Unilac Inc. Any such requirement would have been unnecessary as it would have been unlikely that a shareholder would have depreciated his shareholding in Unilac Inc. by detaching it from the corresponding share of Nestlé.

This structure was dismantled in May 1985 when the shares in Unilac Inc. were detached and redeemed at par.

Examples of income or dividend access schemes

Waterford Glass/Wedgwood plc

At the time of the acquisition of the UK based Wedgwood group by the Irish Waterford Glass group, an income access scheme was adopted. The scheme was adopted principally to enable existing UK resident shareholders of the Wedgwood Group to continue, after its acquisition by

Waterford, to receive their dividend entitlement from a UK source with an attaching tax credit. However, the opportunity was taken to offer existing shareholders of the Waterford Group, some of whom were UK and US resident, the right to take their dividend entitlement from the same source.

The precise mechanics of the scheme involved Waterford setting up a UK resident company, Waterford Wedgwood Holdings (WWH), to acquire Wedgwood. Waterford owned a special share in WWH which entitled it to acquire all the ordinary shares and income access shares. Waterford then exercised the right, conferred on it by virtue of its ownership of the special share in WWH, to acquire the ordinary share capital of WWH in exchange for its own shares. The shares in Waterford and the income access shares of WWH were stapled together by provisions in their respective articles of association.

Existing shareholders in Waterford were granted the right to subscribe for a de minimis amount for income access shares in WWH and were granted the right to elect from which company they wished to receive their dividend entitlement.

SmithKline Beecham

The structure came about as a result of the merger of the US SmithKline Beckman group and the UK Beecham group. The ultimate parent company of the group, SmithKline Beecham plc, is an English company, with both 'A' and 'B' ordinary shares which carry equal voting rights and entitlements on liquidation. The 'B' ordinary shares are stapled to preference shares which the US based SmithKline Beecham group issued on reorganising its share capital prior to the merger. At the time of the merger, the shareholders of the UK Beecham group exchanged all their shares in the company for the 'A' shares (and loan stock) of the newly formed SmithKline Beecham plc while the shareholders of SmithKline Beckman exchanged their common shares for the 'B' ordinary shares of SmithKline Beecham. The existence of the preference shares provides the mechanism through which the US shareholders receive their dividend entitlement directly from the US SmithKline Beckman group. These preference shares, together with the 'B' shares, carry an equivalent dividend entitlement to the 'A' shares.

Hybrid structures

The Unilever structure

This involves two parallel companies, one registered in the Netherlands, Unilever NV, and another, Unilever plc, which is registered in the UK. The shares in both companies are quoted separately and each company has its own subsidiaries.

Both companies are, however, bound together by a so-called equalisation agreement. Under the terms of this agreement, both companies are bound to pay an equivalent dividend, which is fixed by reference to the exchange rate ruling at the date of declaration, and each company guarantees the dividend of the other company. In addition there is a provision that in the event of a winding-up, the equivalent capital distribution will be paid to shareholders of both companies. To the extent that one company has a shortfall in profits (or, in the unlikely event of a winding-up, in the capital available for distribution to its shareholders), then the other company would be required to make a payment under the terms of the equalisation agrement. However, during the period that the equalisation agreement has been in force, it has never been necessary for either company to make an equalisation payment. Furthermore, as there is no certainty that there would be symmetry in the tax treatment of any payments/receipts in the two jurisdictions involved, this structure is of only academic interest to tax practitioners.

Shell

Shell operates through separate Dutch and UK holding companies, which own respectively 60 per cent and 40 per cent of the operating subsidiaries. The shares of both the Dutch and the UK holding companies are traded separately and there is no form of stapling. However, there is a form of income access arrangement between a Dutch subsidiary and Shell Petroleum Inc., the parent of the US sub-group, which enables the latter company to pay its dividend directly to the Dutch subsidiary.

Club Méditerranée

Club Méditerranée is a French multinational which has a subsidiary incorporated in the Grand Cayman. A proportion of the shares in the subsidiary are quoted on the New York Stock Exchange. This subsidiary in turn holds shares in various subsidiaries which are based in the USA, Latin America and the Asia Pacific region. The writer assumes that the tax reason for adopting this structure was to enable a proportion of relatively low-taxed profits to by-pass the French parent company (thus avoiding French tax) and flow directly to shareholders who are based outside France. Clearly there would be important commercial and non-tax reasons for such a structure, eg the need to raise finance for the continued expansion of the group as well as the desire to raise the group's international profile.

This type of structure, involving a separately quoted subsidiary with a minority of outside shareholders, was particularly popular with Australian/NZ based multinationals, with the subsidiaries being quoted in Hong Kong. However, the relatively low rating which these shares attracted resulted in a number of cases in the decision to buy out the minority shareholders (often amid considerable controversy).

Conclusion

Structures such as these, by diverting income directly to shareholders and in so doing enabling it to by-pass one or more jurisdictions, overcome the problems which would arise where income flows through jurisdictions with incompatible tax systems. Even where the tax systems are not inherently incompatible, income flowing through a tax jurisdiction is likely to attract another layer of taxation, which in some cases can be significant. Consequently a structure which provides a means of by-passing one or a number of jurisdictions is likely to afford significant tax savings.

As the European Single Market becomes a reality, the different, and often incompatible, tax systems of the member states will represent a constraint on European multinationals as these are inevitably tied to one or other tax system. In view of the unlikelihood of a harmonisation of tax systems within Europe in the short to medium term, it is likely that Pan-European multinationals with shareholders drawn from a number of member states will increasingly adopt such structures as a means of reducing their cost of capital.

The major disadvantage of these structures lies in their complexity. In addition, there is also the risk that anti-avoidance legislation may be introduced to prevent their use, as it was in Australia. It is for this reason that most structures of this kind have provisions enabling them to be unwound after the expiry of a relatively short period. This complexity, may not only conceal hidden risks for the shareholders, but also comes into conflict with the commercial requirement for the market to be able to understand and evaluate the shares.

Part II

Principles of international tax planning

6
Overseas Expansion, Investment and Acquisitions

Overseas expansion

Usually the first step in the expansion of a business into overseas markets will come about through the planned or unplanned development of export sales. As stated in Chapter 1, the mere export of goods into an overseas country is unlikely to have any direct tax consequences, as without a presence in the country any liability is unlikely to be enforceable in any event. This is because it is a fundamental principle of international law that one country will not assist another in enforcing its revenue laws and in these circumstances the country in which the exporter is based is unlikely to assist the importing country in enforcing its liability. However, like all fundamental principles this is subject to erosion with the development of political and economic groupings such as the European Community and other trading blocs.

Export sales will provide an indication of the potential of an overseas market and this may lead to a decision to try to develop the market further. A company may take a positive decision to develop a particular market and, as a consequence, take the initiative in trying to identify and appoint an agent. On the other hand, the company itself may not identify this potential and an entrepreneur based in the overseas market may approach the company with an offer of his services as an agent. If unplanned, the appointment of an overseas agent is likely to represent the first step on the slippery slope to creating a taxable presence in that country. Prima facie, an agent would represent a taxable presence in the majority of countries and it is for this reason that the OECD Model Double Taxation Convention contains a specific let-out where a company carries on business in another country 'through a broker, general commission agent or any other agent of an independent status, provided that such persons are acting in the ordinary course of their business'. However, the OECD Double Taxation Convention expressly states that an agent who does not have independent status represents a permanent establishment. Inevitably there will be a tension between the commercial requirement so to define the relationship between a company and its agent as to limit the scope for possible future misunderstanding and the need, for tax purposes, to be able to demonstrate the independent status of the agent.

Overseas investment

In theory, there is an optimum structure for outward investment by a multinational although the particular structure will depend on the tax system of the country in which it is based. Likewise, there must be an optimum structure for inward investment into a particular country. However, in practice such structures may be difficult to identify. For example, a multinational investing in the US may have taken the view that the use of a dual-resident financing vehicle (in order to obtain effective relief for the same interest expense in both the US and the UK) was unlikely to be a viable option in the medium to long term, as it was likely to result in the almost immediate introduction of anti-avoidance legislation. With hindsight, the structure operated successfully for a number of years and anti-avoidance legislation appeared on the statute book only some two years after an editorial article had appeared in the *Financial Times* criticising the practice.

Identifying the (apparently) optimum structure for outward investment should be an easier task for the finance director or tax manager of a multinational based in a country with a relatively high level of outward investment, as there will be a wide body of practical experience and information on which to draw. However, this optimum structure may well need to be modified to take into account the particular circumstances of the group. Assessing the optimum structure for inward investment into a country is a much harder task because it is often difficult to identify the organisations or firms (or more particularly the person(s) within them) with this expertise. Once an appropriate structure for inward investment has been identified, it is then necessary to try to integrate this with the optimum structure for outward investment. As it is often not possible to integrate completely the two structures, it will be necessary to make compromises and adapt the structure accordingly. By way of an example of this process, the optimum structure for outward investment by a UK-based multinational will often involve owning the overseas investment through a Dutch holding company. Ownership through a Dutch holding company will enable such a group not only to 'pool' high and low rates of overseas tax in order to maximise relief for double taxation but also to defer tax in respect of any capital gain which would otherwise arise on the eventual disposal of the investment. However, because of the possible introduction of a limitation of treaty benefits clause into the recently renegotiated US/Netherlands double tax agreement, such a structure may be considered to carry too high a risk that it may result in the denial of the benefit of any double tax agreement in relation to US investments and, as a consequence, direct ownership may be the favoured option.

Business entities and their recognition

The optimum structure for inward investment into a particular country may involve the use of unfamiliar types of business entity. For example, investment in Germany often involves the use of silent partnerships. Where unfamiliar types of business entity are incorporated into a structure in this way, it is essential to know how such an entity is viewed for tax purposes in the investor's home country as this will determine how the income is treated in his hands.

Whether a foreign entity is a corporation or partnership under US revenue law depends on evaluating whether it has more corporate than non-corporate characteristics. As both partnerships and corporations involve carrying on business together with associates and with a view to dividing the profits, this evaluation will focus on other factors which are characteristic of corporations; these are:

(1) continuity of life;
(2) limited liability;
(3) centralisation of management;
(4) free transferability of interests.

The domestic law of the foreign entity will be relevant for the purpose of this analysis.

In a Revenue ruling on whether a UK unlimited liability company was a partnership or a corporation under US law, it was held to be a partnership because it lacked the corporate characteristics of free transferability of interests as well as limited liability. It is a matter for conjecture as to whether an unlimited liability company, with free transferability of interests, would be a partnership or a corporation under US law.

Branch v subsidiary

Undertaking an overseas trading activity through a branch rather than through a subsidiary incorporated in the country in question is likely to have different tax consequences. For example, in the UK a branch operation of a foreign company will be subject to corporation tax at the full rate, whereas a UK-based subsidiary of a foreign parent may enjoy a lower effective rate of tax. This will be the case where the foreign parent company is based in a country which has entered into a double tax agreement which provides for the UK to refund a proportion of the tax credit.

In other countries, a branch operation may be more favourably treated. In a country with a classical system of taxation, profits generated by the subsidiary of an overseas parent will attract an element of double taxation. The first incidence will be at the corporate level and the second incidence will take the form of a withholding tax on distributions, although possibly at a reduced rate under the terms of a double tax agreement. Because a branch cannot make a distribution, it would avoid this second charge in the absence of specific legislation intended to put branches on a similar footing to subsidiary companies. A number of countries, including the US in 1986, have introduced a branch profits tax for this reason. (Switzerland is one of the few countries with a classical tax system which has not introduced a branch profits tax.) This tax is designed specifically to ensure that a branch is subject to a tax which is equivalent to the withholding tax which a dividend paid by a subsidiary would attract. A branch profits tax usually operates by deeming the profits of the branch to have been distributed at a certain point in time, which is when the tax applies. This deeming provision may have the perverse effect of putting a branch in a worse position than a subsidiary company. This would be the case where a branch was deemed to have distributed its profits despite the fact that the activities of the branch were expanding and it needed funds to finance this expansion. As a consequence, a branch operation would have to account for branch profits tax before a subsidiary company would have suffered any withholding tax because it would not have made a distribution in such circumstances. However, the precise operation of this form of tax will depend on the domestic legislation of the country in question.

Another distinctive feature of the tax treatment of a branch operation is that because a branch is not a distinct separate legal entity, it cannot receive charges from the head office in respect of central overheads, interest or royalties, in the same way as a subsidiary. It is for this reason that the OECD Model Double Taxation Convention of 1977 provides in Article 7 (business profits) that 'in determining the profits of a permanent establishment, there shall be allowed as deductions expenses which are incurred for the purposes of the permanent establishment, including executive and general administrative expenses so incurred, whether in the State in which the permanent establishment is situated or elsewhere'. The US Treasury Department's Model Income Tax Treaty of 1981 specifically extends the provision to include research and development expenses, interest and other expenses. The UN Model Double Taxation Convention, on the other hand, specifically prohibits the deduction of expenses of this kind, except for interest in the case of a bank.

Under a system of worldwide taxation, the losses of an overseas branch are likely to be fully deductible against profits generated in a company's country of residence, or elsewhere. This means that the initial costs of overseas expansion will be eligible for tax relief, where these result in losses. However, when the branch operation becomes profitable, if it is subject to a lower effective rate of tax in the host country than prevails in the home country, there is an incentive to convert the branch operation, at that stage, into a locally resident company whose profits will be taxable in the home country only when repatriated by way of dividends. The conversion of a branch into a local subsidiary can often be effected on a tax-free basis in the overseas country, although not invariably so. However, the 'home' country's tax system may well contain provisions for an exit or toll-charge to apply in such circumstances. This exit charge may be calculated either by reference to the loss relief originally granted or alternatively by reference to the value of any goodwill transferred by the branch to the overseas company on conversion.

Groups/consolidated filings

Although the majority of countries have provisions in their legislation to allow the offset of profits and losses within a domestic tax group, such provisions are by no means universal. Where there are grouping provisions, the definition of what constitutes a group is likely to vary from jurisdiction to jurisdiction. As a rule, only locally incorporated companies may be included within such a tax group. However, the UK is an exception to this rule in that it permits a foreign incorporated company which is resident in the UK to be included within a tax group. Australia, which introduced grouping provisions in the recent past, exceptionally does not require the ownership of an Australian group to be held through a local parent company. However, most countries will recognise a group for tax purposes only where the shares in the various subsidiaries are owned by a local parent company. This will often have the effect of bringing the shares in any subsidiary company, which is within such a tax group, within the charge to tax in respect of any capital gain arising on their eventual disposal. However, against this potential disadvantage of grouping must be weighed the advantage of having the ability to offset losses against profits within the jurisdiction concerned and, as a consequence, of only paying tax on the net profits generated.

In addition to requirements as to the ownership structure, definitions of the percentage shareholding required for inclusion within a tax group vary from jurisdiction to jurisdiction, as do requirements as to whether indirect ownership qualifies for inclusion within a group; the Japanese tax system was unusual in that, until 1992, it did not permit so-called second-tier subsidiaries to come within a tax group. Some countries extend the definition of a tax group to allow the inclusion of consortium companies. However, these definitions will often be hedged around by anti-avoidance provisions intended to prevent the creation of contrived tax groups whose purpose is to channel tax losses to some other beneficiary, outside the true economic group. For example, the UK has anti-avoidance provisions of this kind, which, although originally introduced to prevent the exploitation by shipping companies of the rules relating to tax depreciation, can have the effect of breaking up any tax group where shares are issued with unusual rights to participate either in profits or in the proceeds of liquidation.

Divisionalisation

Where a country does not permit the consolidation of taxable profits and losses by a group of companies, the possibility of conducting, often diverse, trading activities through a single, divisionalised company should be considered. There are, in any event, other commercial reasons why such a structure may be attractive and these have led a number of multinationals to adopt it despite the existence of grouping provisions in their domestic tax legislation. Multinationals with divisionalised structures of this kind are common in the UK, which has well-established group relief provisions in its tax legislation.

A divisionalised structure involves separate activities, usually with separate management and often a distinctive trading name, being undertaken as a separate part of a single company. So far as the general public is concerned, the use of trading names by the individual divisions serves to maintain their separate identities and disguise the actual legal position, namely that they are dealing with a single legal entity. A disadvantage of operating through a divisionalised structure is that the risks of the individual divisions are not insulated within separate limited liability companies and, as a consequence, may spill over and contaminate other divisions within the company. If a conventional structure had been adopted, with each activity undertaken by a separate company, a catastrophic risk suffered by one of the companies within the group would not necessarily damage the rest of the group. Against this, it is argued that it is increasingly unrealistic to imagine that a multinational with a high profile would be able to 'walk away' from the problems of a subsidiary in such circumstances and that a divisionalised structure simply gives legal recognition to this fact of commercial life.

Tax base

In a large number of countries, especially in continental Europe, the tax base is linked to a company's 'statutory' accounts. Thus the revaluation of an asset which is reflected in the accounts is likely to give rise to an immediate tax liability. This contrasts with the position in countries which adopt a similar convention to the UK, under which the accounting treatment of an item of income or expenditure will have, at best, only a persuasive influence on its tax treatment. In this latter category of countries, tax statute and case law usually determine the basis on which taxable profits or losses are calculated as the statutory accounts of a company are drawn up in accordance with accounting principles which are not influenced by tax considerations.

A striking feature of tax systems which follow the Anglo-Saxon model is the distinction which they draw between capital and revenue items. This distinction derives from revenue law and is not influenced by the accounting treatment of the items of income or expenditure under consideration. This distinction is of particular relevance in those jurisdictions, such as Singapore, which do not tax capital gains. Despite the fact that this distinction originally derived from the UK's revenue law, the basis on which it has been interpreted and applied varies from jurisdiction to jurisdiction. Indeed in a recent landmark decision in the case of *Lawson (HMIT) v Johnson Matthey plc*, the House of Lords, overturning the decision of the lower courts, held that £50 million paid by the taxpayer to the Bank of England in connection with the disposal of the shares in its banking subsidiary (for £1) represented a payment of a revenue nature because it had been made to preserve the trade of the parent company which would have suffered as a consequence of the failure of its banking subsidiary. The lower courts had held that the payment of £50 million had been an inducement to the Bank of England to acquire the shares in the subsidiary company for £1 and could not be severed from that transaction; accordingly the payment was of a capital nature. This demonstrates that the question of whether a payment is of a capital or revenue nature is an issue which is fraught with difficulty, both for tax practitioners and lawyers alike.

Under the US tax system, revenue law determines whether a payment should attract dividend withholding tax, regardless of whether or not the payment actually represents a dividend from a commercial or company law standpoint. This can result in unrelieved double taxation where a payment is characterised as a dividend for US tax purposes and withholding tax applied as a consequence, but from a company law standpoint the payment in question is treated differently and this governs the tax treatment of the item in the country of receipt.

This concept should not be confused with the concept of a constructive dividend, which is a feature of a number of tax regimes with high rates of withholding tax and applies where the whole, or a proportion, of an inter-group payment is considered excessive and accordingly it, or the part which is considered excessive, is disallowed as a deduction on the basis of the arm's length principle. Once a payment has already been made to a recipient in another country and the tax authorities subsequently disallow it, it is logical that it should be recharacterised as a dividend. A constructive dividend can result in possible double taxation, where the tax authorities in the country of receipt disregard the recharacterisation of the payment and tax it on the basis of its original characterisation. Indeed the recharacterisation may occur only after the tax liability of the recipient company has been finalised.

Differences in tax bases result in an increased 'entry' cost into an overseas market as an investor must not only understand these differences, even if only in broad outline, in order to evaluate the effective rate of tax but must also monitor, on an ongoing basis, the different tax treatment in various countries of expenditure such as marketing or research and development, which may be being controlled centrally. The European Commission is eager to harmonise tax bases in order to reduce the 'entry costs' for small and medium-sized businesses who wish to take advantage of the opportunities offered by the Single Market. The lack of enthusiasm of certain of the larger groups of companies for this particular proposal stems, no doubt, from their perception that the differences in tax base, apart from representing a barrier to trade to potential competitors, offer attractive opportunities for international tax planning. As an example of such an opportunity, certain countries allow relief for interest payable (regardless of whether or not it is actually paid) whereas other countries tax interest only when it is received. Consequently it is possible to take advantage of this asymmetry in the tax treatment of interest in order to obtain a tax deferral (because the interest payable will be eligible for relief in one country without a corresponding tax charge arising in the other).

Tax holidays, incentives and grants

Whereas tax havens levy little or no direct taxes, certain countries which, in principle, impose direct taxes grant particular industries or types of activity an exemption from tax in order to promote their development. A number of developing countries offer such tax holidays, especially to manufacturing or labour-intensive industries.

It is usual for developed countries to offer more targeted tax incentives to businesses, especially those in the financial services sector, in order not only to develop the skills of their workforces but also to integrate their economies more fully with other economies in the region. Examples of this are the Singaporean incentives for operational headquarter centres and the Irish incentives for Dublin financial services centre companies. Possibly the best-known tax incentive offered by a European country is the Irish manufacturing relief, which provides for manufacturing activities to be taxed at a reduced rate of 10 per cent. The definition of manufacturing for the purpose of this relief is also surprisingly wide, including as it does software development.

Other countries offer more restricted tax incentives such as reliefs for export sales or additional allowances for expenditure incurred in respect of research and development.

Whereas tax holidays and tax incentives are instruments of fiscal policy, some countries provide cash grants to promote investment. Grants of this kind often prove an expensive form of subsidy as they are payable in advance and regardless of the future profitability of a particular project. In order to make such grants even more attractive, they are sometimes disregarded for tax purposes so that tax allowances for capital investment are calculated on the gross cost, before deduction of any grants.

Losses

The availability of tax losses for carry forward within a tax-paying group may indicate inefficiencies in tax planning (although more usually it simply demonstrates the limitations of tax planning in an unpredictable and uncertain commercial environment). This is because tax losses simply represent deductible expenditure for which immediate relief is not available. Not all countries permit the carry-back or the indefinite carry forward of tax losses, in which case it is essential to ensure that, where they cannot be relieved in the short term, they are preserved for carry forward or otherwise absorbed. Depending on the jurisdiction, a variety of techniques are available to 'freshen up' tax losses so as to prevent their expiry. These techniques range from the injection of permanent or temporary capital (to reduce interest costs in the underlying subsidiary), to a reduction in the rate at which tax depreciation is written off. So far as temporary capital is concerned, this may take a variety of forms depending on the jurisdiction, and may include the use of redeemable participating preference shares to soak up the subsidiary's interest expense until the losses have been fully absorbed, at which time the shares are redeemed. Although most countries' transfer pricing legislation will prevent the granting of interest-free loans to companies based outside their jurisdiction, the UK permits such loans, by concession, where the subsidiary in question is loss-making.

A possible means of utilising future tax losses accruing in another jurisdiction is by transferring the residence of the loss-making subsidiary to a country which recognises tax groups so as to absorb the subsidiary's tax losses within such a tax group. Although it is usual for the residence of loss-making subsidiaries to be repatriated to the country of residence of a group's parent company, it may be possible to transfer the residence to some intermediate country in which other profit-making subsidiaries are resident. The commercial justification for the transfer of a company's tax residence may arise from the need for the management function of the loss-maker to come under the control and supervision of another management team, based in the other jurisdiction. Although a number of countries either have administrative controls or impose toll-charges on the transfer of a company's residence to another jurisdiction, not all countries have controls which prevent or penalise the importation of a loss-making company's residence. However, where there are no such controls, the importation of a loss-making company's residence in this way is likely to provoke the revenue authorities into critically reviewing the residence status of other companies within the group.

Where a tax loss cannot be utilised within a jurisdiction and a strategy is being developed to absorb it elsewhere, ideally this strategy should aim to absorb the loss in a high-tax jurisdiction. This simply reflects the general principle of international tax planning that relief for expenditure should be obtained, so far as possible, in high tax rate countries.

Local taxes

In addition to taxes at the federal or national level, some countries levy taxes at the state or local level. Because these taxes apply at lower rates than national taxes, inevitably less attention is paid to tax planning in relation to them. However, the interaction of state or local taxes presents the same conceptual problems (and opportunities) as are present in the broader international arena. Where state or local taxes are levied on different bases from the federal or national tax, this will inevitably raise compliance costs because it will be necessary to monitor and allocate expenditure and prepare separate computations, among other things, on a state by state basis.

Property investment

Most tax systems differentiate between active and passive property investment. Active investment is often referred to as property dealing or trading (or in US terminology, effectively connected with a business) and as such will usually follow the general principles governing the computation of taxable income and the deductibility of interest which apply in the domestic tax regime.

Gains realised by an overseas resident in respect of passive property investment are usually subject to a separate capital gains tax regime where there is such a regime. Indeed, the OECD Model Double Tax Convention specifically reserves the taxing right in respect of gains arising from property investment to the country in which the property is located. Most countries do not voluntarily forgo taxing rights which have been conceded to them under an international convention, and as a consequence they impose tax on gains arising from the disposal of property within their jurisdiction. However, the UK is unusual in that it does not tax such gains where they accrue to an overseas resident, despite having a separate capital gains tax regime. In jurisdictions which do not levy taxes on capital gains, such as Hong Kong and Singapore, gains arising from passive investment in property may escape tax entirely.

Where a country taxes gains arising from the disposal, by an overseas resident, of passive investment in property, this charge to tax is sometimes extended to include gains arising from the disposal of a domestic or overseas company whose principal investments are property located in that country. This extension in the tax charge is intended to prevent non-residents from 'enveloping' their property interests in domestic, or sometimes offshore, companies and avoiding tax by disposing of the company/ies instead of disposing of their property interests directly. The US Foreign Investment in Real Property Tax Act (FIRPTA) of 1980 is an example of such an extension in the tax charge to include gains arising from the disposal of indirect investment in US property. FIRPTA, in the first instance, deems all gains or losses realised by a non-resident from the disposal of a US real property interest to be US business-connected income. It then extends the definition of a US real property interest to include an interest in the shares of a US company which is a 'US real property holding corporation'; broadly speaking, this includes any company whose US real property interests equal or exceed 50 per cent of its fair market value. In order to provide for the effective enforcement of the tax, FIRPTA imposes not only a requirement on the purchaser of US property to withhold tax from the purchase price but also detailed reporting requirements. The commentary to the OECD Model Double Tax Convention specifically states that the relevant article would not permit the assimilation of shares in a property holding company to property. The introduction of FIRPTA is an early example of the US Government's willingness to resort to the practice of overriding double tax agreements.

Other countries such as France and Spain charge tax annually on a multiple of an assessed rental value where property is owned by a company based in a tax haven. Although the primary purpose of this form of tax charge is to ensure that second homes owned by non-residents (who may or may not rent them to other non-residents) make some contribution to the domestic exchequer, it has the effect of limiting the options to use offshore entities for the ownership of property in a wider range of circumstances.

Overseas acquisitions

When making an initial investment, an investor will have a complete range of options as to how to structure that investment. Where, on the other hand, an investor acquires an existing business or businesses, these options are likely to be restricted by decisions already taken by the original investor in his initial structuring of the business(es). Accordingly the sale and purchase negotiations are likely to give rise to the same conflict between the interests of the purchaser and the vendor as is encountered in a purely domestic situation.

Acquisition of assets or shares

By acquiring assets, as opposed to shares, the acquirer can restore the options that would be available to an original investor, subject to the proviso that he may be acquiring goodwill or other intangible property for which no or only limited tax relief may be available. Apart from the general commercial benefit of not assuming any hidden contingent liabilities, the advantage to the purchaser of acquiring assets is that future tax depreciation on these assets will be based on their full market value. However, the sale of assets is likely to result in the vendor suffering tax, directly or indirectly, not only on the recapture of tax depreciation but also on any capital gains arising from the sale of the assets. In addition, there may well be transfer taxes associated with the sale of assets. Where there are tax losses which would not be available for carry forward by a purchaser, it may be desirable to use these, if possible, to offset any tax liability which would arise by virtue of the sale of the assets. However, losses carried forward are unlikely to be able to shelter the purchaser or vendor from any transfer taxes that may be involved. (Until recent court decisions and the publication in 1987 of rulings by the tax authorities, the acquisition of 100 per cent of the shares in a French company was likely to be regarded by the French tax authorities as a constructive liquidation of the company and, as a consequence, would have been treated as an acquisition of the underlying assets.)

On the other hand, where shares are acquired tax in respect of the capital gain may be avoided where the vendor is resident outside the country of the investment (and he either is not taxed or can avoid or defer a charge to tax in his country of residence). This is because the majority of countries do not tax capital gains arising from the sale of shares in a domestic corporation where the sale is by a non-resident. As previously stated, this may not be the case where the domestic corporation's principal investments are real estate in that country. The commentary to Article 13 of the OECD Model Double Taxation Convention specifically states that 'such gains (arising from the alienation of shares in a company) are, therefore, taxable only in the state of which the alienator is a resident'.

In summary, although the majority of countries do not tax gains arising from the alienation by a non-resident of domestic shares, it would be usual for the provisions of a double tax agreement to grant relief from such a charge where it was imposed. Although the US does not currently tax these gains, legislation has been proposed which would have had the effect of taxing such gains in the hands of a foreign shareholder who owns 10 per cent or more of the shares in a US company. However, although this proposal has not been enacted, it remains a possibility in the current US climate. If such a charge is imposed, it is interesting to note that the UK/US double tax agreement would provide no protection from it, as it does not follow the OECD Model Convention on this point.

Where shares are being acquired from a resident shareholder in a country with a classical tax system, any capital gain which he receives in respect of his shares will usually reflect the underlying goodwill within the company. If the net assets (as opposed to shares) had been acquired, this goodwill is likely to be taxed both within the company and then again in the hands of the shareholder when received by him. Thus by arranging for the shareholder to receive this gain directly, one layer of tax will be avoided although the underlying company will still have a contingent liability which will arise only on the eventual disposal of the goodwill at a profit.

Where the host country has adopted a fully integrated tax system, it would clearly be preferable for any gain to be recognised at the initial, corporate level so that the tax base of the asset is stepped up while the tax suffered will be available to the shareholder as a credit. On the other hand, if the tax system is only partly integrated this decision will be more complex.

Certain countries allow acquisitions to be effected on a tax-free basis where the shareholder of the target company receives shares in the acquiring company in exchange for his shares. Such a tax-free exchange of shares usually represents a tax deferral because the shares in the acquiring company will acquire the base cost of the shares in the target company and, as a consequence, the liability will arise on the ultimate disposal of those shares. Tax-free share exchanges of this kind are often hedged around by a variety of restrictions; for example, that no part or only a very limited part of the consideration received by the shareholder should be represented by assets other than full equity shares. Sometimes these restrictions prevent the exchange of foreign shares from qualifying for tax-free status under a share exchange of this kind. However, the US does not apply such a restriction, although it is fair to say that tax-free reorganisations involving non-US corporations have been relatively uncommon because of a reluctance on the part of US domestic shareholders to accept foreign shares as part of a share exchange. One of the objectives of the European mergers directive is to permit such tax-free share exchanges between companies in different member states in order to promote the restructuring of European industry.

Preserving tax losses

Where a company with tax losses is acquired, it is essential to ensure that the change in ownership of the company will not automatically result in a loss of the right to carry forward these tax losses. Whereas in some countries the change of ownership of a company may result in the automatic expiry of any tax losses, it is more usual for the entitlement to the tax losses to be withdrawn only where there is both a change in the ownership of the company and a significant change in the activity of the company or in the way in which it is conducted. This latter condition inevitably introduces a subjective element into any evaluation of the likelihood of the losses continuing to be available for carry forward after the acquisition of the company. In these circumstances, it is essential to review the domestic tax law, including tax cases and administrative rulings, in the light of the acquiring company's commercial plans for the target company or group prior to the acquisition. Where there is a risk of the losses not being available for carry forward, the possibility should be considered either of delaying the recognition of these until after the change of ownership has occurred (by such techniques as reducing the rate of tax depreciation claimed) or of absorbing the losses by acquiring assets, instead of buying shares.

Acquisition of international companies/groups
Where the operations of the target company or group are themselves international in scope, the possibility of subdividing the acquisition into various distinct elements should be considered. For example, it may be preferable to structure the acquisition of the target group's activities in one jurisdiction as an acquisition of assets, whereas the activities in another jurisdiction could be acquired by purchase of the shares of the company undertaking them. Where this occurs the attribution of the overall consideration to the various constituent elements of the acquisition is likely to be a complex matter. However, by dividing an acquisition into various constituent elements at the outset, it may be possible to restructure the target group and to integrate it into the acquiring company or group in a way that may not be possible if attempted after the acquisition. This is particularly so as it may be possible either to avoid altogether or to withstand any challenge from the revenue authorities as to the correct amount of the consideration which should be attributed to one or more elements on the basis that the price represented an arm's length price agreed between unconnected parties.

Allocation of the consideration
A number of countries have powers under their domestic tax legislation to reattribute and reallocate the consideration where they can show that the existing allocation has been motivated essentially by tax considerations and is not justified by other commercial considerations. The US has only recently introduced such a provision.

Even where a country's domestic tax legislation permits the reallocation of the consideration in the case of a domestic transaction, it does not inevitably mean that in the case of an international acquisition, it can challenge the allocation of the consideration where this is across a number of jurisdictions. For example, where the businesses being acquired have operations in Hong Kong, Singapore, the US and Japan, it may not be open to the Singaporean revenue authorities to attribute a greater or lesser proportion of the overall consideration to the Singaporean business than had been provided for under the terms of the agreement. Where a composite consideration was being broken down over its constituent elements in this way, this point would clearly need to be checked in relation to each and every jurisdiction involved.

Financing investments and acquisitions

To the extent that a company or group does not have surplus funds out of which to finance an overseas investment or acquisition, it will have to borrow these. To a large extent the decision as to where the company or group borrows these funds will be within its own discretion. For example, the parent company or subsidiary based in the same jurisdiction may borrow the funds and use these either to acquire or to invest directly in an overseas investment. Alternatively, an overseas subsidiary based in the same country as the target company or in a third country may effect the borrowings.

The main tax considerations involved in deciding where to borrow funds are the availability of interest relief and the rate of tax at which this is applicable. Ideally the borrowings should be effected in a country with a high rate of tax, so as to reduce the after-tax cost of borrowings. It is better still if relief can be obtained for the same interest expense in two countries at once, although this has become more difficult following the widely publicised introduction of anti-avoidance legislation in both the US and the UK. This anti-avoidance legislation was aimed at preventing the use of dual-resident financing companies to effect acquisitions. The dual-resident company was resident in the US by virtue of being incorporated there and accordingly could be included in the US consolidated filing; in this way, relief was available in the US for the interest expenses which it incurred. The company was also resident in the UK because it could be demonstrated that this was where it was 'managed and controlled' and, as a consequence, effective relief for the interest expense was obtained through the UK's group relief provisions.

An investor will be concerned not only with the question of the availability and rate of interest relief but also with the question of whether there will be sufficient taxable profits to absorb the interest deduction (this concept is commonly referred to as taxable capacity). Clearly it would be undesirable to structure borrowings through a country with a high rate of tax, if the group's profits were unstable and could prove insufficient in the long term to absorb the deduction.

So far as concerns the availability of interest relief, the home country or intermediate jurisdiction may well deny or restrict this where the borrowings have been incurred for the purpose of financing overseas investment. On the other hand, the host country is likely to seek to restrict the amount of interest relief available by the application of thin capitalisation or earnings stripping provisions. Even where relief is available, the detailed technical rules governing it invariably present pitfalls for the unwary.

Another important consideration in the financing of acquisitions and investments is the question of the currency in which the borrowings are to be denominated. By borrowing in the same currency as the underlying investment, the interest expense will be matched by future income receivable and, as a consequence, there is no exchange risk. However, because of a lack of symmetry in tax systems, this apparent solution to the problem of the exchange risk may lead to a tax trap. The UK tax system is an obvious illustration of the problem arising from this so-called tax fragmentation. Because the UK tax system focuses on transactions rather than the economic substance, any gain arising from the eventual disposal of the investment will give rise to a tax liability whereas any corresponding loss arising on repayment of the loan will not be eligible for relief (the reason for this is that the loss arises from a capital transaction which, because it is a liability, falls outside the scope of the capital gains tax regime). This asymmetry in the treatment of differences on exchange can be reduced or avoided where the overseas subsidiary borrows externally in local currency; however, as already explained, this can lead to other problems. (See Chapter 8: *International Financing and Overseas Finance Companies.*)

7
Tax Havens

Tax havens represent an ideal refuge in which to shelter profits from tax regimes with relatively high rates of tax. This is self-evident to taxpayers and revenue authorities alike and, as a consequence, the latter invariably circumscribe the use of tax havens by a wide range of anti-avoidance measures.

The growth in international trade and developments in telecommunications have led to a substantial growth in the business, and number, of tax havens. Improved communications have resulted in increased levels of activity and a consequent reduction in unit costs and this has led to the wider use of tax havens as their services have become more affordable. The marketing efforts of the tax havens themselves and the financial institutions based in them have further reinforced this process.

What is a tax haven?

Tax havens are commonly divided into three categories. These are:

(1) the zero-tax haven;
(2) the low-tax haven; and
(3) the tax haven which imposes tax at normal rates but grants exemption, or other preferential treatment, to certain categories of income.

The first two categories are made up predominantly of small economies (often British colonies, or dependent territories which may or may not have become independent) whose revenue needs are met by indirect taxes, or by a combination of indirect taxes and low direct taxes. These territories have used the absence, or low rates, of direct taxes in order to promote investment in their financial sectors. In certain jurisdictions (eg Bermuda), the high level of indirect taxes means that the costs of doing business there are high. Where this is the case, such jurisdictions have tended to attract high value-added work, with a low ratio of costs to income, eg captive insurance, reinsurance or investment management.

Because jurisdictions in categories (1) and (2) levy little or no tax, they have not, as a rule, been able to enter into any double tax agreements. This is because it is necessary, in order to enter into double tax agreements, for one jurisdiction to be able to offer the other jurisdiction a reduction in rates of tax in return for the other jurisdiction offering a similar reduction in respect of its own taxes. Tax havens in categories (1) and (2) have, by their nature, nothing to offer in this bargaining process.

Jurisdictions which come into category (3) are often not tax havens in a strict sense as they levy direct taxes at normal rates whilst relieving from tax certain types of income. The Netherlands, with its participation exemption, and Ireland, with its manufacturing relief and its incentives for the International Financial Services Centre in Dublin, are examples of such jurisdictions. Because these jurisdictions levy direct taxes, they have been able to negotiate often extensive networks of double tax agreements. In the case of such jurisdictions, the main emphasis of international tax planning has been to take advantage either of specific incentives, such as the manufacturing relief in the case of Ireland, or of the network of double tax agreements by treaty shopping. This practice has led to increasing anti-avoidance measures which have the effect of denying the benefit of the agreement to any party who has interposed a company or other entity which is considered to be a mere conduit. (See Chapter 12: *Anti-avoidance Legislation in the International Arena*.)

Apart from anti-treaty shopping provisions, most developed countries have anti-avoidance legislation aimed at preventing multinationals from forming 'letter-box' or 'money-box' companies in tax havens; the US's sub-part 'F' and the UK's controlled foreign company legislation are examples. However, in order not to inhibit genuine commercial activities, anti-avoidance legislation of this kind often contains exemptions for activities with genuine commercial substance. The UK's controlled foreign company legislation contains such an exclusion in respect of so-called 'exempt' activities. In order to ensure that only bona fide commercial activities come within the scope of this exemption, certain conditions are laid down, including the requirements that the foreign company should occupy suitable business premises and employ sufficient personnel in the business.

Certain categories of company, such as the domiciliary company in Liechtenstein and Switzerland, suffer from inherent structural weaknesses because the domestic legislation in their country of incorporation requires that they should have minimal substance in order to qualify for the relevant tax benefits. This requirement may cause them to fall foul of any anti-avoidance legislation in the investor's country of residence.

The revenue authorities of developed countries are well aware that developments in telecommunications have opened up the possibility of companies which are nominally managed in tax havens being effectively controlled from their jurisdiction and, as a consequence, are looking increasingly critically at structures which include tax haven companies. Accordingly, it is essential to ensure that these operations do have sufficient substance to withstand investigation. Whatever the definition of corporate residence, whether it is the 'purposive' definition which has regard to the place of effective management of a company or the arguably formalistic definition, adopted by the UK, which has regard to the place where a company is managed and controlled and places considerable emphasis on the forum at which policy decisions relating to the company are taken, the identity, authority and residence status of the directors are likely to be crucial factors. Whilst the practice of appointing 'nominee' directors to the board of tax haven companies may delay scrutiny by the revenue authorities, it is unlikely to provide protection in the event of an investigation. As a separate issue, it is widely thought that jurisdictions whose company law derives from the UK cannot have boards of directors consisting entirely of nominees because the definition of a director is so wide as to embrace 'shadow' directors.

Even the less developed countries have anti-avoidance legislation, where goods or services are bought and sold within a multinational group, aimed at preventing the transfer of profits out of their jurisdiction and into a tax haven, through artificial pricing arrangements.

The attributes of a tax haven

In order to attract business in the first instance, a tax haven must have the necessary commercial infrastructure, which will include:

(1) an adequate supply of suitably qualified staff in order to enable transactions to be executed efficiently;
(2) good quality communications. It must be possible to communicate information in a businesslike manner. Even where communications are of an otherwise high standard, severe weather conditions may result in seasonal disruptions. Furthermore, for general ease of communication, it is advisable to ensure that the selected tax haven is in a suitable time-zone. It is with good reason that the client base of the Caribbean tax havens comes mainly from the US, that of European-based tax havens from Europe and South Africa, and that of Hong Kong, Vanuatu and the Cook Islands from the Asia Pacific region;
(3) a suitable legal and regulatory environment. It is important that the tax haven has a developed and established legal system which will ensure that property rights are respected and obligations are honoured. In addition, its financial sector should be sufficiently regulated so as to minimise the risk of loss to investors in general. As a rule, the better established the tax haven the greater will be its concern to safeguard its reputation and this will be reflected in its regulatory environment and in the costs of doing business there; and
(4) freedom from exchange control restrictions, at least insofar as concerns overseas investors. However, where there are exchange control restrictions, these should be administered in such a way as not to

interfere with commercial activity or impose too high a compliance cost on such activity.

Political stability

Any company transferring part of its assets to another jurisdiction will want to be satisfied that its assets are not at risk in that other jurisdiction. However, this consideration may be less important where business is simply being transacted through a particular tax haven, with the profits subsequently being channelled to another more secure jurisdiction.

In order to allay possible concerns about their political stability, certain tax havens have enacted legislation enabling companies incorporated there to transfer their domicile to some other jurisdiction, either at will or sometimes only in a time of emergency. Other tax havens, often those enjoying a reputation for political stability, have legislation which enables companies incorporated elsewhere to transfer their domicile into their own jurisdiction. However, it is now becoming increasingly common for tax havens to introduce legislation which enables a company incorporated in another jurisdiction to transfer its domicile into their jurisdiction whilst at the same time permitting a company incorporated there to transfer its domicile to another jurisdiction. These provisions have the dual advantage of allowing the tax haven in question to attract business at the expense of any other tax haven which may be suffering from political instability while at the same time putting to rest any concerns which potential investors may have about the long-term political stability of their own jurisdiction. The transfer of a company's forum of incorporation in this fashion is commonly referred to as 'redomiciliation'.

The redomiciliation of companies, however, raises a number of complex tax and legal issues. In particular, it is thought as a matter of international law that a company may change the forum of its incorporation only if the jurisdiction from which it proposes to move has laws which permit this, and equally the jurisdiction to which it proposes to move permits such a transfer. Where a company proposes to transfer its domicile and hold assets outside either jurisdiction, it is important to ensure that the jurisdictions in which the assets are located do not treat them as having been disposed of (with all the tax consequences which that may entail) by virtue of the redomiciliation. As a further point, where a company which proposes to transfer its domicile is itself a subsidiary of a foreign parent, it is important to determine how the law of the country in which the parent company is resident views the redomiciliation of companies. If it is regarded as a deemed dissolution of the original company, followed by a new incorporation, this could give rise to a substantial capital gain or could require consents which may not be forthcoming.

Confidentiality

Although of less relevance to multinational companies, a large number of users of tax havens are concerned to ensure that their affairs remain confidential. In order to reassure users or potential users, a number of tax havens have introduced confidentiality laws imposing criminal penalties on bankers or other professional advisers who betray their clients' confidence. The most notable example of such a jurisdiction is Switzerland, which introduced its confidentiality laws in 1934 at a time when the assets of German Jews were being expropriated and Germany had introduced draconian criminal penalties aimed at anyone who was guilty of economic 'crimes'.

Although there are clearly circumstances when it is legitimate to protect the confidentiality of someone's business affairs, there are equally circumstances when it is illegitimate to so do. The developed countries, in particular, have been concerned to protect themselves from the abuse of the confidentiality laws of certain tax havens.

The abuse of confidentiality

The developed countries have shown increasing concern at the use of tax havens to launder the proceeds of organised crime, examples of which are the laundering of drug money, insider trading and the financing of terrorist activities. The US has been especially active in using its economic muscle to persuade Switzerland and the Caribbean islands, among others, to enter into Mutual Legal Assistance Treaties. In addition, the EC is proposing to introduce directives which will make insider trading and money laundering criminal offences. Other international organisations, such as the Group of Seven leading industrial nations, have addressed this issue. Jersey, Gibraltar, Guernsey and the Isle of Man, among others, have all introduced legislation which requires disclosure by banks where drug trafficking offences have been committed. Depending on the jurisdiction, other offences such as insider trading are brought within the scope of similar legislation. Switzerland recently enacted legislation making it a criminal offence to assist in money laundering.

In relation to insider trading, certain countries, such as the UK with section 212 of the Companies Act 1985, have introduced legislation which has the effect of denuding shares of value where there is a suspicion that the shares have been the subject of insider trading. This is achieved by placing restrictions on dividend rights and the right to vote or to transfer the shares unless there is full disclosure of the identity of any party with an interest in the shares.

Development of tax havens

Apart from the complete absence, or reduced rates, of direct taxes, tax havens have to be in a position to provide the overseas investor with a variety of services. The principal of these is a corporate entity which combines considerable flexibility with the minimum compliance requirements and yet will be recognised in other jurisdictions as having a separate legal personality and as affording the protection of limited liability to its shareholders.

Traditionally the business of tax havens has been built on the provision of companies. Where individuals are the ultimate owners of these companies, trusts are often interposed in order to avoid taxes and also to achieve a greater degree of confidentiality for the ultimate beneficiaries. Such companies are often used to buy goods and services from some third country for resale at a substantial profit to a company owned by the person or persons responsible (possibly indirectly) for creating the structure. In a recent case in the UK, an individual who engaged in this type of activity was charged with and convicted of fraud; it is likely that other developed countries would take a similar line. Some commentators take the view that the Revenue would not have pursued a charge of fraud, or alternatively would not have been able to sustain such a charge, had all the commercial activity taken place outside the country of residence of the ultimate beneficiary of the structure, and a company based in a tax haven been used to purchase goods from some other country for re-sale at a substantial profit in yet another country. This will obviously depend on the relevant legislation in the country(ies) under consideration. So-called reinvoicing companies are particularly popular in jurisdictions, such as Hong Kong, which have a high level of commercial activity, as this lends credibility to their activities.

That such re-invoicing companies are a common feature of tax haven operations is evidenced by the case of *Agip (Africa) Ltd v Jackson*. The facts of this case were that a senior employee formed an overseas company which issued invoices, purporting to be for the provision of oil, to the company which employed him. He himself authorised the payments to the overseas company. When his employing company discovered the fraud, it sought to countermand payment but its attempt was unsuccessful. Accordingly, it sought to obtain restitution of the amount in question from the managers of the overseas company through which the payment was made. The courts held that the equitable remedy of tracing was open to the victim of the fraud and that the company managers were liable. Although this case has been widely reported and has caused concern in tax havens, the company managers were only held liable for the payments which were made once they had been put on notice that the activities of the company, which they managed, were fraudulent, and not for prior payments. Clearly, the requirement to preserve confidentiality in relation to client affairs means that it is not possible to conduct any enquiries which may otherwise indicate that the contemplated activity is fraudulent.

That the provision of companies and the ancillary services associated with them constitutes the 'bread and butter' work of the majority of tax havens is evidenced by the speed with which Guernsey and Jersey, two relatively developed financial centres, introduced their own exempt company legislation when there was a risk that they would lose this business to other jurisdictions.

A tax haven that is successful in attracting this business can extend and develop its infrastructure so as to provide a more sophisticated range of services. Examples of services offered by tax havens which are relevant to multinationals are contained in the section of Chapter 8 which deals with overseas finance companies and Chapter 9: *Special Categories of Offshore Company*.

Offshore investment funds

Offshore investment funds are often set up and managed in tax havens. The investment income of such funds will be tax free, apart from any withholding taxes suffered in the country of source, as will any capital gains accruing to the fund. Whilst distributions to investors are likely to be free from any withholding or other taxes in the jurisdiction in which the fund is based, the tax position of a corporate or individual investor will be determined by the country of residence. The UK, for example, has specific anti-avoidance legislation to prevent its residents from converting income into capital gains. Other countries also have anti-avoidance legislation to prevent their residents from deferring tax by investing in so-called roll-up funds which are based in tax havens.

As part of the process of creating a single European market, the EC has issued directives relating to undertakings of collective investments in transferable securities (UCITS). A fund which meets the requirements of these directives and is based in a jurisdiction which is within the EC may be marketed throughout the EC. In the absence of tax harmonisation within the EC, any UCITS which is to be marketed throughout the EC is likely to be based in a jurisdiction where the investment income and capital gains are subject to little or no tax; Luxembourg, Ireland and Gibraltar are such jurisdictions.

Offshore pension schemes

Where a multinational enterprise employs third country nationals, it may be desirable for them to participate in a pension scheme which is constituted outside the jurisdiction in which they perform the duties of their employment. Indeed it may be desirable, not just for third country nationals, but also for nationals of the jurisdiction in which the parent company is resident to participate in such a pension scheme where they work abroad. This would be the case if a pension scheme based in their home country is not subject to an advantageous tax regime or they are excluded from participating in it by virtue of their employment abroad, or where the employee wishes to retire to another country on termination of employment.

Financial services for specific jurisdictions

In addition to the services described in Chapters 8 and 9, tax havens often develop financial services which are aimed specifically at taking advantage of tax concessions or anomalies in the legislation of neighbouring jurisdictions. In the context of the UK's tax legislation, such services include the provision of offshore trusts for non-UK-domiciled individuals as well as offshore companies through which such individuals are employed to undertake duties outside the UK. The development of the so-called roll-up funds is a classic example of a financial service which aimed at exploiting an anomaly in the UK's tax legislation. Roll-up funds converted income into capital and allowed even taxpayers of modest means to avoid tax. As soon as the UK's revenue losses started to become significant, anti-avoidance legislation was introduced. It is interesting to note that after the introduction of composite rate tax in the UK (in effect a form of deduction of tax at source) in respect of bank and other interest, the Guernsey and Jersey authorities are understood to have discouraged the aggressive marketing in the UK of Guernsey and Jersey bank deposits which pay interest gross.

At a more sophisticated level, the recent takeover activity aimed at 'unbundling' the assets of UK-based target groups has frequently involved a company based in a tax haven as the potential takeover vehicle. Because of anomalies in the UK's tax legislation, such companies can dispose of the target group's assets without attracting the capital gains tax liabilities which a UK-based entity would incur.

Conclusion

Essentially the financial sectors of tax havens provide administrative services, with remuneration dependent to a large extent on levels of activity/transactions. Although the professionals based in particular tax havens may have developed considerable expertise in relation to outward investment from a neighbouring jurisdiction, this is not inevitably so. Often their experience derives from transactions which other clients have effected and, as a consequence, it reflects the quality of those clients. Accordingly where a multinational is being advised to structure transactions through a tax haven, it is essential to analyse fully, at the outset, the tax consequences of the proposed structure from the perspective of the tax regime not only of the parent company, but also of any intermediate company as well as those of any operating companies which will, directly or indirectly, make payments to the tax haven company.

8
International Financing and Overseas Finance Companies

International financing

Debt v equity

According to conventional wisdom, a classical tax system discriminates against equity investment and in favour of debt. This is because under such a system, tax-deductible interest payments attract only one incidence of tax in the hands of the recipient whereas equity investment will result in tax at the corporate level and then again in the hands of the shareholder on distribution of the profits. On the other hand, in the case of a full imputation system, there is no such discrimination against equity investment because there is in effect only one incidence of tax.

According to this reasoning, a partial imputation system or a system which provides a partial form of shareholder relief will discriminate against equity investment in the same way as a classical system. This is because such tax systems accept by implication the principle of double taxation which underlies a classical system, the only differences being of degree and mechanics. However, the extent of this discrimination will depend on the shortfall between the relief which the shareholder receives and the effective burden of tax suffered at the corporate level.

Because a country with a tax system which imposes a heavy burden of double taxation on corporate profits is also likely to impose high marginal rates of personal tax, there will be an incentive to incorporate in order to obtain the benefit of a tax deferral by avoiding these high rates of personal tax. This is because the rate of corporation tax will be set at a level which takes account of the double taxation implicit in the system and, inevitably, this will be lower than the marginal rate of personal tax so as to avoid being excessively confiscatory. Accordingly, incorporation may enable profits to be generated and to compound at the lower rate of corporation tax. Anti-avoidance legislation aimed at preventing the hoarding of profits within companies may restrict the benefit of any such deferral, although legislation of this type has proved difficult both to administer and enforce. The incentive to incorporate will be influenced by a judgment as to the efficacy or inefficacy of any such anti-avoidance legislation. Where capital gains are taxed on a more favourable basis than ordinary income, the investor will be able to realise his investment and be taxed only on the gain under this regime and so avoid full double taxation at maximum marginal rates of personal taxation which would result from withdrawing profits directly from the company.

Financing overseas expansion

Although these considerations will be relevant when considering the form which a group's external financing takes, other considerations will apply in the case of internal financing, ie, when deciding whether to finance an overseas subsidiary with equity or by way of loans.

The decision as to whether to finance an overseas subsidiary by injecting capital or by means of borrowings usually lies with the head office treasury and tax departments. The basic tax principle which applies is that capital should be introduced into subsidiaries in low or no tax countries whereas the funding requirements of subsidiaries based in high tax countries should be met by borrowings. In this way the 'endowment' profit attributable to the introduction of capital will accrue and compound in a low or no tax country, whereas interest will be incurred and relieved in a high tax country, provided that it is in principle deductible. There may be circumstances when general commercial considerations dictate that this rule is not followed. For example, where in addition to a tax holiday a developing country also provides committed funding in order to encourage certain types of investment. Despite the fact that the terms on which such funds are made available may not be particularly favourable, it may be desirable to take advantage of external borrowings as these will reduce the group's exposure to political risk, provided that they are not supported by guarantees.

Where a group finances overseas expansion out of borrowings, it should not only ensure that relief is available in principle for its financing costs but should seek also to maximise this relief. It is clearly advantageous to structure borrowings so that full, effective relief is available for the costs of finance in a country with a 50 per cent rate of tax, rather than one with a 30 per cent rate.

Where funds are on-lent to a subsidiary, most countries' tax systems will require the loan to bear a commercial rate of interest and this will have the effect of transferring the costs of financing the original borrowings to the subsidiary. Where, on the other hand, the original borrowings are used to finance an increase in the capital of the subsidiary, the costs of finance will be borne by the parent company. However, some countries either deny completely or limit the tax relief which is available for the costs of financing overseas investment. Either apart from, or in addition to, limitations on interest relief, the tax legislation of a country may include regulatory controls which restrict a company's ability to acquire overseas investments or increase the share capital of existing subsidiaries. Such regulatory controls are designed to prevent the erosion of the country's tax base which would result from the shifting of taxable profits into other jurisdictions.

It may be desirable for an overseas subsidiary to effect borrowings directly in order to finance its expansion. In a number of jurisdictions, external borrowings enjoy the following advantages.

(1) There is less likelihood of these being challenged under thin capitalisation rules, especially if the loans are not guaranteed.
(2) There is less likelihood of the interest rate being questioned in the light of transfer pricing regulations.
(3) Under the terms of certain double tax agreements, external bank borrowings are treated preferentially, with either no, or a reduced rate of, withholding tax applying.

Hybrid financial instruments

These financial instruments combine characteristics of both debt and equity. This can result in a particular instrument being characterised as equity for general commercial purposes, such as capital adequacy requirements in the financial sector, whilst at the same time being characterised as debt for tax purposes. As an example of such an instrument, there have been reports in the financial press recently that a UK bank is to issue undated, subordinated debt which can be converted later into preferred stock, at the option of the bank. For the purpose of assessing the bank's capital adequacy under new international guidelines the undated subordinated loan would be regarded as capital, whilst for tax purposes the interest would be deductible until such a time as the subordinated debt was converted into preferred stock. By financing its capital by tax-deductible interest payments, the bank's financing costs will be reduced. It is understood that this proposed financing structure will be unaffected by anti-avoidance legislation the UK has introduced in the Finance (No. 2) Act 1992 which will have the effect of treating interest payments on certain perpetual, floating rate notes as distributions of profits (and hence not ranking as deductible interest).

The above example demonstrates how a hybrid financial instrument can be treated differently for a variety of purposes within the same jurisdiction. However, in an international context the same instrument can be treated differently for the same purpose. This is often referred to as a cross-border hybrid and this asymmetry provides an opportunity which can be exploited in tax planning. Thus it may be possible to finance an overseas operating company by using a hybrid instrument which is regarded as debt and hence generates a tax deduction in the host country while avoiding tax in a home country which operates an exemption system because it is regarded there as equity. Even if the home country applies a system of worldwide taxation, this technique may still be useful as a means of averaging double tax relief where the hybrid instrument is held by a company based in an intermediate jurisdiction which treats it as equity and accordingly does not tax the return on it. (See pages 127–128 in Chapter 10: *Holding Companies and Co-ordination Centres* for a full description of this.)

Tax absorption lending

Where an international lender receives full credit for withholding tax suffered (ie can absorb the withholding tax) in respect of interest paid to him, the withholding tax will not represent an additional cost to him. (This disregards both the possible cash flow loss which would arise where the withholding tax is withheld before the lender's normal tax payment date as well as additional compliance costs involved in obtaining credit for this tax.) However, by granting a credit for withholding tax the lender's country of residence will be forgoing revenue. This loss to the country of residence's exchequer will be particularly acute where a withholding tax is applied to the gross amount of the interest payment despite the fact that the lender has incurred costs in financing the loan. This is illustrated below:

Example 1

Interest receivable (gross)	100	(10 withholding tax)
Interest payable	80	
Net profit on loan	20	
Other income	10	
Net profit	30	
Tax thereon at 33%	10	
Less double tax relief	(10)	
Domestic tax payable	–	

In this example the tax attributable to the net profit (after financing costs) on the loan is 6.7, with tax of 3.3 attributable to the other income. Because the full withholding tax of 10 is offsettable against this 'combined' liability, effectively the exchequer in the lender's country of residence is subsidising the loan.

Where, on the other hand, an international lender receives no credit for withholding tax suffered, he will want the borrower to compensate him by paying a correspondingly higher rate of interest. This can be illustrated by adapting the earlier example:

Example 2

Interest receivable	111
Less irrecoverable withholding tax	(11)
	100
Less interest payable	80
Net profit on loan	20
Other income	10
Net profit	30
Domestic tax payable	10

In both examples 1 and 2, the net of tax profit is 20. However, the borrower's financing costs in example 2 will have increased considerably. As a consequence, the borrower will try inevitably to borrow from a lender in the same position as the lender in example 1. This is likely to result in a firming of the interest rate in response to the increase in demand for credit from such sources. This will automatically result in a sharing of the tax advantage between the borrower and the lender.

Under the terms of certain double tax agreements with developing countries, relief may be available for tax 'spared' (see Chapter 3: *Double Taxation and Double Tax Agreements*, page 35) in relation to certain categories of approved loan (usually to finance the development of a country's infrastructure). Under such arrangements, the borrower is entitled to a credit as though tax had been withheld even though no tax is actually withheld.

Certain countries, such as Belgium, give double tax relief by way of a percentage deduction, regardless of the amount of withholding tax actually withheld. Both tax-sparing arrangements and such percentage deductions have a similar effect and stimulate tax absorption lending.

In response to tax absorption lending, a number of countries have introduced restrictions on the credit available to banks and other financial organisations for withholding tax suffered in respect of overseas loans. These restrictions usually have the effect of limiting the credit for withholding tax by reference to the commercial profit on the loan. This involves offsetting a commercial cost of finance against the interest receivable from an offshore loan, calculating the attributable tax and, where this is sufficient, crediting the withholding tax accordingly. This restriction prevents any excess withholding tax from being absorbed by any tax liability attributable to other income of the business.

International leasing

Recent years have seen the rapid development of leasing as a means of financing the acquisition of assets. In its initial phase, a very favourable tax environment gave a considerable stimulus to this development. In particular, the lessor as owner of the assets (the lessee being the user) was often entitled to generous tax depreciation allowances and investment tax credits. The availability of tax depreciation allowances to the lessor, who was often simply a passive investor, enabled him to benefit from a significant tax deferral. This was especially so in an era of high tax rates, with particularly high marginal rates of personal taxes. This led to the development of consortia of individuals, often limited partnerships, who in return for providing finance obtained a substantial part of the tax benefits of the arrangement.

Although it is often difficult to determine who receives the effective benefit of the tax relief associated with the acquisition of assets, tax authorities were concerned at the ability of leasing arrangements to transfer, at least a part of, this benefit to an essentially passive investor. However, in the case of certain tax exempt organisations, such as local or municipal authorities, the ability of the financier to obtain the benefit of these allowances (even if, in effect, these were shared with the lessee under the terms of the lease) clearly represented an unintended cost to the exchequer. As a consequence, a number of revenue authorities sought to restrict the ability of leasing arrangements to transfer to an essentially passive investor the tax benefits associated with asset acquisition and, furthermore, to deny or restrict tax benefits where the lessee was exempt from tax in their jurisdiction. Although a number of tax jurisdictions have been successful in persuading the courts to accept distinctions between various categories of lease in order to achieve this objective, others have introduced specific legislation to achieve this end. This legislation has often borrowed and imported into tax legislation distinctions made by accounting standards. Of particular relevance is the distinction between operating and financing leases. However, not only do the accounting definitions differ between jurisdictions, but not all jurisdictions have adopted this practice. Some have introduced into their tax legislation distinctions between operating and financing leases which do not depend on distinctions which exist in accounting standards.

Where one country grants the tax benefits associated with the acquisition of assets to the legal owner and another grants tax benefits to the user of the assets, this offers the opportunity to obtain two separate allowances in respect of the same asset; so-called double-dip leases. These are cross-border leases which deliberately exploit this lack of symmetry in order to attract entitlement to tax benefits in two separate jurisdictions and thus reduce the overall financing costs associated with asset acquisition. As a further refinement of this concept, there is the so-called triple-dip lease, which relies on two jurisdictions recognising different parties as the legal owner of an asset and granting them the tax benefits attributable to the ownership of assets in their respective jurisdictions, whilst the third jurisdiction grants these benefits to the user. Two jurisdictions may recognise different parties as the legal owner of an asset because of different interpretations of the same set of circumstances. For example, the subtle distinctions involved in the definitions of hire purchase and conditional sales lend themselves to conflicts of law and offer opportunities for tax planning. The commentary on Article 12 of the OECD Model Double Tax Convention addresses this issue and recommends that a credit sale agreement and a hire purchase agreement should be treated as outright sales. These definitions usually involve:

(1) hire purchase: title passing on the exercise of an option at the end of the period of hire;
(2) instalment sales: the upfront transfer of title, with payment being effected by instalments;
(3) conditional sales: the upfront transfer of title, although it may revert in certain circumstances.

Because of the considerable complexity involved in cross-border leasing in general, and double- and triple-dip leasing in particular, it is usually only relevant to items of significant capital expenditure, such as ships, aircraft and oil rigs.

As tax considerations are at the heart of leasing transactions, leasing agreements contain detailed tax indemnities which relate to the tax position of the lessor. It is therefore important for a lessee to understand the tax position of the lessor, especially where cross-border leasing is involved.

A number of countries impose withholding taxes on leasing payments. The OECD Model Double Tax Convention of 1977 sought to address this problem by including such payments within the definition of royalties, contained in Article 12. However, although the OECD takes the view that such payments should be exempt from withholding tax in the country of source, this position is not accepted by a number of countries. Although it may be possible for the lessor to avoid a withholding tax by contriving to have a permanent establishment in the country of residence of the lessee, such an arrangement is likely to involve a significant compliance cost. (By having a permanent establishment, the lessor may suffer tax only in respect of his net profit and the lessee may be absolved of the requirement to withhold tax.)

However, where the lessor has suffered withholding tax in respect of the gross amount of lease rentals received, it is unlikely that this tax will be fully relievable, either in principle or in practice, as the net profits from the overseas leasing activity will be unlikely to be sufficient to absorb it. It should be borne in mind that the imposition of a withholding tax on the gross amount of a cross-border lease payment means that the element of the payment which represents a return of capital will suffer tax. Any withholding tax should apply only to that element of the leasing charge which represents the financing charge, although there is no justification for treating lease payments differently from interest payments.

So far as anti-avoidance legislation is concerned, it is not clear why the revenue authorities should concern themselves where an inbound lease has benefited from tax advantages in another jurisdiction, although there is Australian case law as well as decisions of the US tax authorities which indicate that they do. In the case of an outbound lease, both the UK and the US limit the tax benefits available to the lessor. A number of other countries have similar legislation.

Differences on exchange

Most tax systems have evolved over a period of time when international trade was the exception rather than the rule. It was only as a result of the growth in international trade and investment that the problems arising from differences on exchange became a common feature of the business environment. This was particularly so during the recent era of floating currency rates and liberalised exchange controls.

In view of the well-publicised failures of UK accounting standards to cope with the complexities of accounting for differences on exchange, it is not altogether surprising that tax systems have failed, in the main, to cope adequately with these same problems. The rules governing the treatment of differences on exchange often result in a lack of symmetry in the taxation of gains and losses. This lack of symmetry arises because the majority of tax systems focus not just on the individual corporate entity but beyond that on specific transactions.

When the tax system focuses on specific transactions, there is a possibility that two transactions, which should in essence be considered together, will be taxed on different bases, ie asymmetrically. The UK tax system provides the most graphic examples of the anomalous results which such an approach can produce. For example, a UK company which borrowed $10 million (when £1 was $2) to acquire a US business for the same amount would face a tax liability (ignoring indexation) of 33 per cent of £5,000,000, ie £1,650,000, if it sold the asset some years later, for the same original price, when the £ was $1. Although the gain on the sale of the asset would be matched by an equal and opposite loss on repayment of the loan, the gain on the disposal of the asset would come within the scope of the tax regime applicable to capital gains (and losses), whereas the loss on the loan would fall outside it (because a loan is not an asset, and the regime only applies to assets). Furthermore, this loss would fall outside the definition of a trading expense and so would not qualify for a deduction under that heading. The narrow focus of tax regimes in general and the consequent lack of symmetry in the treatment of differences on exchange is often referred to as tax fragmentation.

There is a relationship between the interest yield of a currency and the market's expectation of its future exchange rate which is reflected in the forward currency markets. Thus where one currency offers an interest yield which is 5 per cent higher than that of another currency, this reflects the market's expectation that the former currency will depreciate by 5 per cent against the latter. However, tax fragmentation often results in a disregarding of this fundamental relationship and a difference between the tax treatment of the interest and the movement on exchange, affecting the value of the principal, which is its counterpart. Whereas interest may be taxed as income, the difference on exchange may fall to be taxed as a capital gain/loss. To the extent that income and capital items are subject to tax at different effective rates, tax fragmentation presents both opportunities and pitfalls.

Another instance of tax fragmentation arises from the accounting convention (which is usually followed for tax purposes) which requires losses to be provided for whether realised or not, yet recognises gains only on realisation. This means that it was possible to enter into two separate transactions which, although cancelling each other out in commercial terms, would generate a tax deductible loss at the year-end while the corresponding gain would not attract a tax charge. This type of transaction is usually referred to as a straddle because the two transactions remain open over the company's financial year-end. However, the majority of developed countries now have anti-avoidance legislation to defeat this tax planning technique.

New financial instruments

With the abolition or relaxation of exchange controls in a number of countries, suddenly the world has become the financier's oyster. Tax law has not managed to keep pace with the rapid development of new financial instruments and this results in opportunities and risk at both the domestic and international level.

The function of these instruments can be defined as transferring a price or credit risk or enhancing liquidity. These instruments are often referred to as 'derivatives' because their value is linked to that of a primary instrument such as a debt asset or liability. Interest rate swaps, collars, floors and similar instruments provide for payments between parties to be determined by reference to notional principal amounts. However, there can be a considerable variety in the precise contractual arrangements in a transaction involving a new financial instrument and these arrangements may affect its tax treatment. For example, payments under the contracts may or may not be netted off, the contracts themselves may involve a financial institution as a counterparty, or a financial institution may simply act as an intermediary.

In the same way that anomalies exist at the domestic level in relation to the tax treatment of differences on exchange, so too are there anomalies in the tax treatment of new financial instruments. Even if the anomalies were eliminated at the domestic level, there would still be opportunities to exploit differences in tax treatment at the international level. These would only be eliminated if the basis of taxing financial transactions were harmonised as this would remove differences at the international level. This harmonisation would inevitably have to extend beyond new financial instruments to encompass the taxation of the primary instruments from which they derive.

At an international level the new financial instruments can be used to redefine interest as discount, so as to avoid withholding tax. Furthermore, the yield on a cross-border loan can be reduced by denominating the loan in a low yield currency, so as to minimise withholding tax, while hedging the exchange risk.

Although there is clearly scope for international arbitrage, the tax law surrounding new financial instruments is inevitably unsettled and until such a time as it has become better defined this will introduce a significant risk into such activity.

Overseas finance companies

Reasons for forming an overseas finance company

The principal tax reasons for forming an overseas finance company are to:

(1) divert profits out of the jurisdiction of the parent company;
(2) extract profits from overseas jurisdictions with relatively high rates of tax;
(3) combine both approaches (1) and (2). Ideally his diversion and/or extraction of profits should be to a tax haven with a nil or, at least, low rate of tax. However, both the jurisdiction in which the parent company is based and the overseas jurisdictions in which the operating companies are based are likely to have anti-avoidance legislation to prevent this.

Apart from the above, there are a number of additional reasons why a group may decide to form an overseas finance company. For example, the group may wish to obtain access to the Eurobond markets in order to raise finance. Because interest on the Eurobond markets has to be paid gross, it may not be possible for the parent or other domestic subsidiary to incur the borrowings directly, as domestic legislation may require them to withhold tax from interest payments to non-residents. As a consequence, it may be necessary to form an overseas finance company in a country, such as the Netherlands, which does not require tax to be withheld from payments of interest to non-residents. This company would incur the borrowings and on-lend the funds throughout the group. Provided that the country in which it was resident had a network of double tax agreements which eliminated or reduced the rate of withholding tax in respect of interest which it received, these would fund its own interest expenses arising from its Eurobond borrowings which could be paid without incurring withholding tax.

Another reason for forming an overseas finance subsidiary is to enable the group to match, in a tax-free environment, transactions which may result in an asymmetrical tax treatment if undertaken in the tax jurisdiction of either the parent company or an overseas operating company. For example, a UK based group may incur a foreign currency denominated borrowing which it seeks to hedge. Whereas a loss suffered in respect of a long term, foreign currency denominated borrowing is likely to be regarded as being of a capital nature and thus non-deductible for tax purposes, a corresponding gain in respect of the hedging instrument may well attract a tax liability. Thus, although the currency exposure had been fully hedged at the pre-tax level, a residual currency exposure would remain at the post-tax level. By effecting the currency hedging in a tax haven, there is no risk of any asymmetry arising in the tax treatment and consequently the costs of hedging will be reduced. Where, as in the UK, there is anti-avoidance legislation which taxes the (income) profits of controlled foreign companies, this arrangement may be ineffective for tax purposes.

Diversion of profits

Where the parent company of a group employs its own capital to form an overseas finance company, this would have the effect of reducing the 'endowment' profit in its home country while at the same time giving rise to an 'endowment' profit in the country of incorporation of the overseas finance company. Where, however, the parent company has to borrow in order to finance the injection of capital into the overseas finance company, the availability of interest relief will be a critical consideration. If interest relief is available, the parent company will have successfully transferred profits out of its home jurisdiction and into a low tax environment. To the extent that the overseas finance company on-lends the funds to operating companies based in other jurisdictions, this may enable profits to be extracted in the form of interest payments from these companies, thus doubling the potential for saving tax. It should, however, be borne in mind that this latter tax saving assumes that the alternative to the overseas operating companies being financed by group lending would be for them to be financed by injections of capital. In the majority of cases, the realistic alternative is for the operating companies to be financed by direct, external borrowings.

Where, on the other hand, no or only restricted relief is available for these financing costs in the home jurisdiction, it is essential that the income which accrues to the overseas finance company is not taxed in the home jurisdiction, as otherwise double taxation would arise.

Most countries have anti-avoidance legislation aimed at preventing the shifting of profits out of their jurisdiction and into a tax haven. This anti-avoidance legislation usually takes the form of regulatory controls, often linked to exchange controls, which either restrict a company's ability to form subsidiaries in certain (tax haven) countries or limit the amount of share capital which they can inject. In addition, most developed countries have anti-avoidance legislation similar to the US sub-part 'F' legislation which is aimed at preventing groups from sheltering profits in low tax jurisdictions. This type of legislation would clearly threaten the profits generated by an overseas finance company.

Extraction of profits

Transfer pricing provisions generally prevent the charging of excessive interest on inter-company loans as a means of extracting profits from the jurisdiction of a host country. Switzerland prescribes maximum rates of interest which apply to such loans and any amount paid in excess of this will not only be disallowed as a deduction for corporate tax purposes but will have withholding tax applied.

In addition, the host country invariably will have rules dealing with thin capitalisation. These are aimed at preventing overseas investors from extracting excessive profits by way of deductible interest payments and so eroding its revenue base. Such rules are notoriously difficult to define because of the relative ease with which external borrowings can be substituted for inter-group borrowings. Whereas some countries' rules only apply to loans from shareholders, other countries encompass any inter-company borrowings and yet others include all borrowings, whether external or inter-group, within their definition.

Where interest is payable to a resident of a country which has entered into a double tax agreement with the host country, a number of countries have rulings which would prevent the practice of treaty shopping. The US has developed the most extensive armoury of anti-treaty shopping rulings (see Chapter 12: *Anti-Avoidance Legislation in the International Arena* for a fuller description). These rulings have the effect of preventing the elimination or reduction of withholding tax where the ultimate beneficiary of the payments is not resident in the treaty partner country.

Characteristics of the ideal finance company location

The following are the principal characteristics of the ideal location for an overseas finance company:

(1) the complete absence or, at least, a low rate of tax in respect of interest and, ideally, other income;
(2) an extensive network of double tax agreements which either protect interest receipts entirely from or, at least, limit substantially any withholding tax applicable in the country of source;
(3) the absence of withholding tax in respect of payments of interest or dividends;
(4) the absence of capital taxes in respect of capital introduced into the company;
(5) the absence of exchange controls or other constraints on the free movement of funds.

Because countries which impose little or no tax in respect of interest or other income (1 above) would not be in a position to negotiate a network of double tax agreements (2 above), it is invariably necessary to combine two jurisdictions in order to achieve the ideal conditions for structuring international financing transactions.

Choice of location

Considered below are a number of locations which, when combined with a traditional tax haven, provide the essential elements for structuring international financing activities. In particular, they provide access to extended networks of double tax agreements which reduce or eliminate withholding taxes on interest receipts whilst the absence, under their domestic legislation, of withholding tax on certain interest payments, allows the profits of the company to be paid on to a low tax or tax haven jurisdiction without attracting a significant tax liability in the intermediate country. As explained previously, any country which has successfully negotiated a favourable network of double tax agreements is likely to levy taxes at fairly high rates itself. It is for this reason that an overseas finance company, resident in such a country, should be able to on-pay, in a tax-deductible form, any interest which it receives to a company based in a pure tax haven. However, it is invariably necessary to leave a margin in charge to tax in the intermediate jurisdiction although the precise amount of this margin of profit can often be negotiated and agreed in advance. The ability to reach an agreement in advance enables financial planning to proceed, free from at least one element of uncertainty. However, increasingly the uncertainty arises out of the tax treatment of interest payments by the country of source, especially where the interest is being paid to an intermediate country and the benefits of a double tax agreement between the country of source and that country are being claimed.

The Netherlands

The Netherlands is the best known location for an overseas finance company. This is because it does not impose any onerous exchange controls and enjoys political and economic stability, being at the heart of the European Community. In addition, it has an extensive network of double tax agreements which eliminate or substantially reduce withholding taxes in respect of interest receipts. The Netherlands does not impose withholding tax on interest payments (except in the case of profit-sharing bonds, the interest on which is treated in the same way as dividends). Although a margin of profit must be left in charge to Dutch tax (which is relatively high), this is subject to prior negotiation with the Dutch revenue authorities. There are defined guidelines which lay down a sliding scale for this profit margin, depending on the levels of income flow. The Dutch revenue authorities will give a binding ruling as to what level of profit accords, in their view, with the arm's length principle. (See Chapter 11: *The Netherlands and Netherlands Antilles in International Tax Planning*, pages 146–147.)

Another interesting feature of the use of a Dutch overseas finance company is that a deduction is permitted for notional interest payable, where the Dutch finance company is the recipient of an interest-free loan. However, the interest forgone is likely to be subject to Dutch capital duty, which is at the rate of 1 per cent.

Switzerland

Like the Netherlands, Switzerland offers a politically stable environment in which to establish an overseas finance company. Switzerland does not apply any form of exchange control. Although it has an extended network of double tax agreements, the terms of the individual treaties are often not as favourable as those of the Netherlands. In addition, Switzerland introduced an anti-abuse decree into its domestic legislation in 1962 to prevent the abuse of its treaty network. The decree was introduced largely to allay the fears of potential treaty partners who were concerned that, by entering into a double tax agreement with Switzerland, they would be inviting investors to engage in treaty shopping.

So far as its implications for the activities of an overseas finance company are concerned, the anti-abuse decree prevents more than 50 per cent of the interest income of a Swiss company being paid out in a tax-deductible form. Accordingly a relatively high proportion of a company's total interest receipts must remain in charge to federal taxes (albeit at the low rate of 9.8 per cent) and cantonal taxes (if applicable). In addition, the Swiss anti-abuse decree requires at least 25 per cent of interest income which has benefited from Switzerland's double tax agreements to be redistributed by way of a dividend. Unless reduced by a double tax agreement, Switzerland imposes a withholding tax of 35 per cent on dividends.

A further disadvantage of Switzerland's network of double tax agreements is that the agreements with Germany, France, Italy and Belgium contain the additional requirement that income received by a Swiss resident company must be subject to full cantonal and communal taxes (in addition to the federal tax referred to above) in order to enjoy the benefit of the agreement. This would have the effect of pushing the tax cost of the structure up to often prohibitive levels, especially when compared with the alternative of using the Netherlands as a finance centre.

Swiss branch of a Dutch company

One way of overcoming the problems associated with the use of either a Dutch or Swiss company is by using a Dutch company with a Swiss branch. The problem associated with the Netherlands is that it taxes profits at a relatively high rate and, as a consequence, has traditionally been used as an intermediary jurisdiction with income flowing in under the protection of the Dutch network of double tax agreements and then, so far as possible, being paid out in a tax-deductible form to a pure tax haven. However, as the profits of an overseas branch of a Dutch company are exempt from Dutch tax, where it undertakes a substantive activity, by using a Swiss branch of a Dutch company the relatively high rate of Dutch tax is avoided. Consequently the branch operation will only be subject to Swiss tax and an advance ruling can be obtained to define the precise scope of this. The profits of the branch are determined in accordance with the arm's length principle under the terms of the double tax agreement between the Netherlands and Switzerland. Accordingly it is necessary to agree a deemed level of branch capital, with a deduction available for notional interest paid by the branch to its head office in respect of other funding. Applying these principles, a low effective rate of Swiss tax can be agreed which often equates to a cost-plus basis.

Because it is a Dutch company which receives the interest income, the rate of withholding tax applicable to the interest paid to it would be governed by the provisions of the relevant treaty with the Netherlands. This avoids the problems associated with the use of the Swiss network of double tax agreements.

Other locations

Belgium, through the use of co-ordination centres, and Ireland, through the use of a company based in the Dublin Financial Services Centre, offer fiscal incentives to encourage the establishment of finance companies. In the Asia Pacific region, Singapore also provides incentives with its operational headquarter centre legislation.

Anti-avoidance and overseas finance companies

There are a number of bases on which the tax authorities in the parent company's home country can challenge the mode of operation of an overseas finance company. The most obvious challenge that can be mounted is to the overseas finance company's residence status. It will be difficult to demonstrate that the company's 'mind and management' is indeed in the chosen overseas jurisdiction if the directors of the company are mere nominees, all of the company's activities are initiated by staff from the head office and, where material, its actions are subject to head office board approval. Although it is unusual for revenue authorities to pursue such a challenge to its ultimate conclusion, this is probably because a challenge under controlled foreign company legislation places greater reliance on objective criteria, rather than the subjective facts of a particular case.

Controlled foreign company-type legislation prevents multinationals from benefiting from a tax deferral or exemption where essentially passive sources of income accrue in a low tax or tax haven, outside the taxing jurisdiction of the parent company. Such legislation typically deems the income of the overseas finance company to be the income of the parent company and taxes it accordingly.

So far as concerns the tax authorities in the host countries, these often have thin capitalisation provisions which deny relief for interest expenses where the borrowings are considered to be out of proportion to the company's capital base. Sometimes such provisions only apply to inter-group borrowings, sometimes they extend to third party borrowings but only where supported by security or guarantees provided by the same group, and in other cases encompass all borrowings.

Where the rate of interest on inter-group borrowings is excessive, invariably this can be attacked under transfer pricing legislation, with the result that a proportion of the payment is treated as a hidden distribution.

In addition, revenue authorities have strengthened their armoury of measures aimed at preventing treaty shopping. These measures range from provisions contained in their domestic legislation to specific anti-avoidance provisions contained in the double tax agreements themselves. Increasingly, double tax agreements are likely to include general provisions limiting the benefits of the agreement exclusively to 'true' residents of the treaty partner countries.

9
Special Categories of Offshore Company

Certain special categories of offshore company are a common feature in the structure of many multinational groups. Apart from serving essentially commercial purposes, which are outside the scope of this book, they fulfil a useful tax function by enabling the group to extract profits from high tax jurisdictions. This category of company is invariably based either in a pure tax haven or in a low tax jurisdiction, outside the jurisdiction of both the parent and operating companies.

The most common types of company which fulfil such a role in an international tax structure are: finance companies (see Chapter 8: *International Financing and Overseas Finance Companies*); captive insurance companies; licensing companies; other service companies.

Active and passive functions

The type of company which has an essentially passive function, for example holding investments, owning intellectual or other property rights or lending money within a group, may be located in any jurisdiction with a suitable infrastructure and an attractive tax climate.

Where the company is to engage in an 'active' function, the choice of jurisdiction will be determined to a large extent by considerations of geography and a detailed analysis of the commercial attractions of the jurisdiction. For example, this will include a review of the availability and quality of the workforce, in terms of the general educational standard and work-ethic, as well as other factors such as the availability and cost of suitable premises. Jurisdictions such as Switzerland, Ireland, Hong Kong and Singapore, with their relatively developed economies, can provide a greater quality and depth of infrastructure than 'pure' tax havens. It is for this reason that they are often selected as suitable bases for companies which perform active functions of some kind.

Anti-avoidance provisions

Most countries in which multinationals are based have anti-avoidance legislation aimed at preventing the use of companies based in tax havens either to avoid or defer tax. Although anti-avoidance legislation of this kind will generally target companies resident in tax havens which receive essentially passive income, it will often cast its net wider and encompass certain types of active company as well. Usually these anti-avoidance provisions operate by deeming that any 'tainted' income accruing to a tax haven company is income of the parent company (see Chapter 12: *Anti-Avoidance Legislation in the International Arena*).

In addition to anti-avoidance legislation in the jurisdiction of the parent company, the host jurisdictions in which the operating companies are based will have provisions of their own to prevent the extraction of profits by way of tax-deductible payments to a company based in a tax haven. Generally speaking, these provisions will impose an obligation on any company which makes certain types of payment (eg interest, royalties or management and technical service fees) to an offshore entity to withhold tax. Sometimes these provisions go beyond simply requiring the paying company to withhold tax and seek to deny the paying company the right to deduct the payment where certain conditions have not been fulfilled. Although most double tax agreements contain provisions which either eliminate the requirement to withhold tax or, at least, considerably reduce the amount required to be withheld, the majority of pure tax havens do not enjoy the benefit of any double tax agreements.

Treaty shopping

For this reason a common feature of international tax planning involves interposing, between the company making the payment and the ultimate beneficiary company in the pure tax haven, a company based in a jurisdiction with a developed network of double tax agreements. It is essential that the jurisdiction in which the interposed company is itself resident does not require tax to be withheld under its own domestic legislation from the type of payment in question. This will enable the amounts received by the intermediary to be on-paid free from withholding taxes to the tax haven company.

As a general rule, neither the Netherlands nor Switzerland imposes withholding tax under its domestic legislation on the payment of royalties. The Netherlands does not impose any withholding tax on interest payments; Switzerland imposes it at 30 per cent, but only on certain corporate bonds and bank loans. Another feature of both the Dutch and the Swiss tax systems which has enhanced their attractions as intermediate locations for licensing companies, and in the case of the Netherlands for finance companies, is the possibility of obtaining an advance clearance from the tax authorities on the level of profit which must be left in charge to tax in their jurisdiction. It would not accord with the arm's length principle for a company to on-pay an amount exactly equal to its income, so an amount of profit must be left in charge to tax in the intermediate jurisdiction. Bearing in mind that the rate of tax in that jurisdiction is likely to be relatively high (otherwise it is unlikely to have been able to negotiate an attractive network of double tax agreements), the taxpayer will clearly wish to minimise the amount of any profit left in charge to tax. The ability to obtain an advance clearance allows the taxpayer to determine in advance the costs involved in adopting a given structure. This is helpful in any exercise in financial planning. An example of a structure which includes such an interposed company is illustrated in Figure 9.1.

Figure 9.1

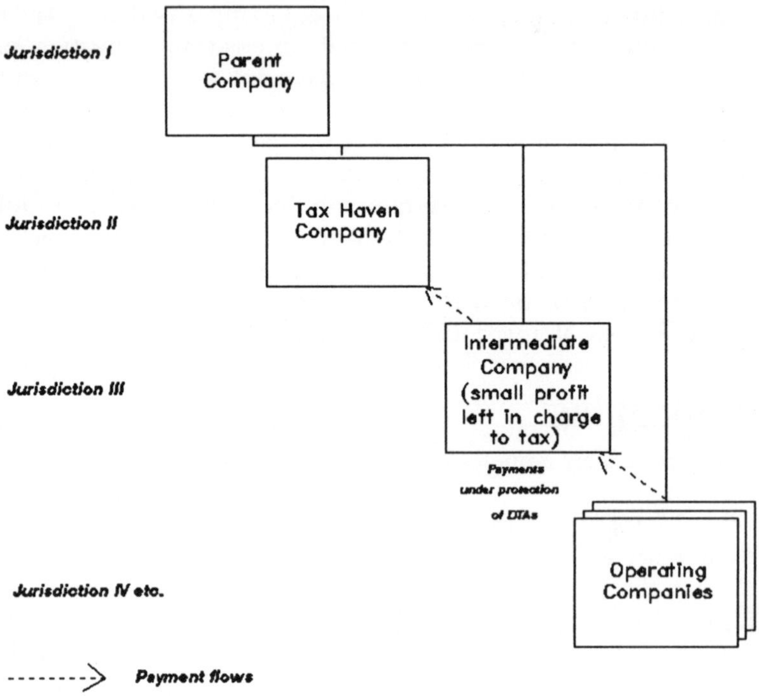

General anti-avoidance

The more sophisticated jurisdictions are likely to attack structures which involve the routing of payments through a jurisdiction which benefits from a treaty network to an ultimate beneficiary company in a tax haven. The basis for such attacks may be in domestic anti-avoidance concepts, eg substance over form or *abus de droit,* which may enable the revenue authorities to disregard the fact that the payment was routed through a jurisdiction which benefited from a double tax agreement and have regard instead to the tax haven, beneficiary company. In addition, the US has sought to include so-called limitation of benefit provisions in any new double tax agreements, which would deny the benefit of any double tax agreement which is entered into by the US to residents of third countries.

The US has taken this process a stage further by incorporating 'treaty override' provisions in its domestic legislation (see Chapter 12: *Anti-Avoidance Legislation in the International Arena*). No doubt other jurisdictions will follow this lead.

Captive insurance companies

A captive insurance company (a captive) is a company which has been formed by an industrial, commercial or financial group of companies to underwrite certain risks of the group. As a general rule, a captive will restrict itself to underwriting the risks of the group. Although some captives do undertake third-party business, this is infrequent because it requires a greater depth of insurance expertise than the majority of groups possess. That expertise to which they have access is often provided by an insurance management company, frequently the subsidiary of an insurance broker, as this is often more economic than the alternative of employing insurance specialists directly.

Commercial rationale for establishing a captive

It is generally accepted that it is only worthwhile for a group to establish a captive if there is sufficient commercial justification, apart from possible tax benefits, for its formation. There are a number of commercial reasons why it may be advantageous for a group to form a captive. These are:

(1) by obtaining direct access to the reinsurance market (ie the wholesale insurance market), a captive may effect considerable savings in a group's insurance costs;
(2) where a group's risk record is above average, this is unlikely to be reflected fully in its external insurance costs because insurance operates on the basis of averaging, ie a pooling of risks, both good and bad. A captive, on the other hand, can reflect in its premium levels the above average risk profile of the group which will be unaffected by the averaging which would result from the inclusion of poorer quality, third-party risks;
(3) a captive can 'smooth' the traditional feast (high premium) and famine (low premium) cycles which are a characteristic of the insurance market;
(4) a captive can insure types of risk for which no 'external' market exists, eg nuclear risks and risks relating to the residual value of finance and other leases.

Where the captive either does not or cannot reinsure the risks, there will have been no transfer of risk from a group perspective even though there will have been a transfer of risk between legal entities. To the extent that a tax deduction is allowed to a company which pays a premium to a captive in such circumstances, all that the group will have achieved is to transform what otherwise is likely to have been a provision for a possible contingency – and as such generally non-deductible – into a tax-deductible expense. Furthermore, by virtue of the fact that it is paid to a company based in a tax haven, the premium income can accumulate gross – or at least subject to very low rates of tax.

For a group with a large number of essentially similar assets, eg retail property or motor vehicles, it may be commercially desirable to self-insure the risks through a captive, because the large number of individual risks would allow the law of averaging to apply. In these circumstances, the captive may bear the run-of-the-mill risks associated with these assets but reinsure any 'catastrophe' risk element, such as a fire in a shop which results in the death of a number of customers.

Before setting up a captive, it is essential to review the relevant legislation in the jurisdictions of the prospective insuring companies to confirm that no restrictions are imposed on transacting so-called non-admitted insurance. Where there are such restrictions, it may be possible to avoid them by insuring in the first instance through a locally based, conventional insurer who then reinsures with the captive; such arrangements are known as 'fronting'. Because the conventional insurer will want a reward for its involvement, fronting will increase the costs involved in operating a captive. It is fair to say that fronting is regarded with suspicion by revenue and other regulatory authorities alike.

Choice of location for a captive

Because few, if any, jurisdictions impose withholding tax requirements on the payment of insurance premiums, captive insurance companies do not need to be located in a jurisdiction which affords treaty protection. Although the US originally excluded premiums paid to Barbadian (US/Barbados double tax agreement) and Bermudan (Treaty on Insurance Taxation and Mutual Assistance in Tax Matters, and Agreement to Exchange Tax Information) insurance companies from the US excise tax payable in respect of insurance premium payments, the US unilaterally withdrew the benefit of these provisions from captives resident in either territory. Accordingly, other tax and commercial considerations will determine the choice of tax haven in which to locate a captive.

One such consideration is that the home country of the parent company may have anti-avoidance legislation aimed at such companies as captive insurance companies but the existence of a double tax agreement between that country and the country in which the captive is located may afford the captive protection from the effects of such legislation. For this reason Ireland is a popular choice of location for the formation of captives among German parent companies, despite the fact that Ireland levies tax at 10 per cent on such companies. (However, it is understood that Germany is in the process of introducing domestic anti-avoidance legislation which would have the effect of withdrawing these benefits.)

Other jurisdictions which combine facilities for captives with the benefits of a low rate of tax and a degree of treaty protection are Cyprus (tax rate 4.25 per cent), Malta (5 per cent) and Barbados (nil).

A variety of other jurisdictions, which do not benefit from any treaty protection, combine facilities for captives with a tax-free environment. In particular, the majority of Caribbean jurisdictions provide these facilities, as do Bermuda, Gibraltar, Guernsey and the Isle of Man.

Because the insurance industry is in general highly regulated, the compliance costs of forming a captive in certain jurisdictions can be considerable. The regulatory requirements in the majority of tax havens are far less onerous, especially where no third-party business is involved, so this is often a compelling reason for incorporating such companies in a tax haven.

Tax considerations

The tax considerations affecting the formation and operation of a captive fall into two categories: those which affect the parent company and those which affect the operating companies.

Anti-avoidance and the parent company

The tax considerations which affect the parent company will centre on the determination of the residence status of the captive and on the applicability of any anti-avoidance provisions relating to the sheltering of profits in tax havens. It will clearly be essential to establish that the captive does indeed have an offshore residence. Invariably, this will involve establishing that the directors of the company are, in the main, resident in the relevant jurisdiction and that real decision-making powers are vested in them and are habitually exercised by them. Where such anti-avoidance legislation is on the statute book, it is likely to apply to any captive. However, in the case of the UK, the effect of the anti-avoidance legislation can be mitigated by ensuring that the captive makes an acceptable level of distribution (within the terms of the legislation). Other jurisdictions may have similar let-outs.

Anti-avoidance and the operating company

There are a number of grounds on which the jurisdiction in which the operating company is based may seek to challenge the deductibility of an insurance premium paid to a captive insurance company. It may challenge the payment on the basis that there has been no real transfer of risk because the risk has remained within the 'economic family' of the group. Where the captive's level of capitalisation is clearly insufficient to meet potential claims which may arise (and no or insufficient reinsurance is effected), the revenue authorities may argue that the premium payment represents a distribution of profits. In addition, they may simply seek to challenge the quantum of any premium payments, possibly by reference to any third party quotations which may be obtainable.

Licensing companies

It generally makes good commercial sense for a group of companies to centralise control over the intellectual property rights of its individual member-companies. The reason for this is that the legal issues involved in protecting such rights are so complex and specialised in nature that it would be impractical and uneconomic to try to disperse this kind of expertise throughout a group.

The next logical step was to centralise the ownership of intellectual property rights in a separate company for which the legal/intellectual property department had managerial responsibility. The tax attractions of owning such rights through an offshore, tax haven company (offshore licensing company) soon became apparent to multinationals and their use became a common feature of international tax planning.

These tax attractions are the possibility of:

(1) making tax-deductible royalty payments from high tax jurisdictions to a low tax regime;
(2) allowing the royalty income to compound at a nil or low rate of tax;
(3) avoiding tax completely in the home country of the parent, where overseas income is subject to an exemption system, or, where a worldwide system of taxation applies, deferring it until the licensing company pays the profits back to its parent company by way of a dividend.

So far as point (3) is concerned, the majority of developed countries have introduced anti-avoidance provisions which deny the benefit of the exemption or deferral to offshore companies of this type. Bearing in mind that a licensing company's activities are fairly limited – although a high level of expertise is required in order to safeguard a company's intellectual property rights, its activities are essentially administrative – the revenue authorities may either probe these in an attempt to suggest that the structure lacks substance or challenge the company's residence status.

So far as point (1) is concerned, the majority of tax regimes (except the Netherlands and Switzerland) impose a withholding tax obligation on the payment of royalties to an offshore entity. It would therefore be necessary for the offshore recipient to benefit from a network of double tax agreements if royalty payments received by it were either to be free from or subject to a reduced rate of withholding tax. As previously mentioned, those jurisdictions which have a developed treaty network invariably levy tax at a relatively high rate themselves, and so it is generally undesirable for the royalty income to accrue and be taxed there. In the circumstances, a structure which is frequently encountered involves a company in a tax haven actually owning the property rights and hence being the ultimate beneficiary of the royalty income. This company in turn grants a licence of all or some of its rights to a company based in a jurisdiction which offers the protection of a treaty network. This latter company will then grant a sub-licence to the operating companies. Such a structure is illustrated in Figure 9.2.

Figure 9.2

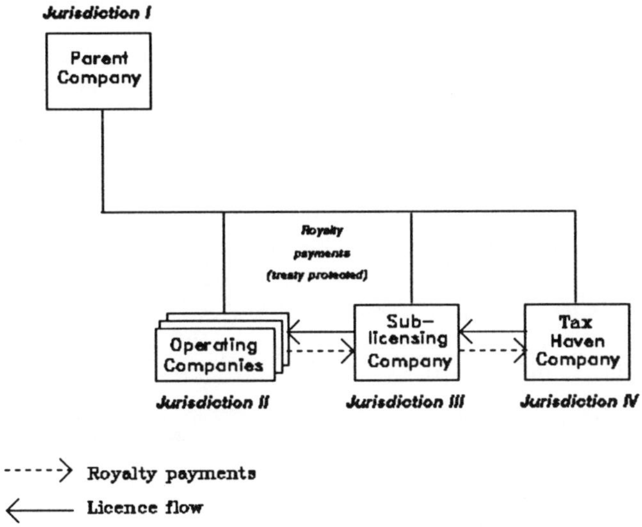

Clearly the use of a sub-licensing company will involve any group in additional costs. Because it is necessary to leave an element of profit in charge to tax in the sub-licensing company, part of these costs will be represented by the tax charge which these profits attract. As the rate of tax is likely to be relatively high, it is important to ensure that the profit element which remains within the sub-licensing company is kept to a minimum. The advance clearance procedures in Switzerland and the Netherlands, referred to previously, allow these costs to be determined at the outset.

Anti-avoidance legislation in the jurisdiction of the operating company will generally include transfer pricing legislation which will disallow the payment of royalties where these can be considered excessive. Indeed the royalty provision contained in the OECD Model Double Tax Convention would deny the benefit of the treaty, where there is a special relationship between the payer and the recipient, to that amount of any royalty payment which exceeds an arm's length rate. The majority of double tax treaties have followed the OECD model on this point. Accordingly, it is essential to be able to justify the royalty rate by reference to commercial criteria, preferably royalty rates paid by independent third parties. In addition to anti-avoidance legislation in the tax field, certain jurisdictions impose other regulatory restrictions, especially exchange control, which require prior approval before any royalty agreement is entered into.

The majority of developed jurisdictions will also have a wide range of anti-avoidance doctrines, ranging from substance versus form and limitation of treaty benefits to specific treaty override provisions which may attack 'conduit' structures. Although the majority of professional advisers are of the opinion that US anti-conduit rulings relating to interest payments apply equally to royalty payments, the IRS has not sought to pursue this line of attack but instead has ruled (Ruling 80-362) that a 'secondary withholding tax' applies to certain royalty payments which ostensibly benefit from treaty protection. The facts of the case were that a citizen and resident of a third country granted a licence in respect of US patent rights to an unrelated Dutch company, in exchange for a fixed royalty, payable annually. The Dutch company in turn licensed a US company, which agreed to pay the Dutch company a royalty based on unit production. Although the IRS accepted that the royalty paid by the US company to the Dutch company benefited from the exemption under Article IX(I) of the US/Netherlands DTA, the IRS held that the royalty paid by the Dutch company to the third country resident retained its character as US source income and, as a consequence, the Dutch company was under an obligation to withhold US tax as there was no double tax agreement between the US and the third country in question.

Despite the growing problems on the tax front, it has become increasingly common for multinationals to transfer their property rights into the outright ownership of a Dutch company for essentially commercial reasons associated with the protection of these rights. Although the royalty income will attract a high nominal rate of tax, the use of gearing and the availability of a deduction in respect of a proportion of the value of the property rights reduces the effective rate of tax. Because the Dutch company has full beneficial interest in the property rights, such a structure is considered to be less vulnerable to attack by the revenue authorities.

However, the transfer of property rights into a licensing company can trigger a variety of tax liabilities including, for example, capital gains tax, transfer and stamp duties. These liabilities may outweigh the discounted value of projected savings from the formation of a licensing company. For this reason, it is often only possible to form such a company when acquiring property rights from third parties or when new rights have only recently been developed or are in the process of development.

Other jurisdictions have included specific provisions in their double tax agreements which provide that the reduced rate of withholding tax is only to apply where the royalties are fully subject to tax in the country of receipt. Germany's agreement with Switzerland contains an example of such a provision. It is essential therefore to check the specific provisions of all relevant double tax agreements before setting up such a structure.

Other service companies

Sales companies

An international sales company is usually formed to effect sales into a particular national or regional market. Ideally it should be resident in a jurisdiction which, apart from subjecting profits to a low rate of tax, can also offer treaty protection in respect of sales into its principal markets. Provided that there is a double tax agreement in force and that the sales company does not need to set up a permanent establishment in a particular market, the majority of double tax agreements will allow sales to be effected into a jurisdiction without the selling company necessarily incurring a liability to tax there. This is because it is usual for a double tax agreement specifically to provide that:

> an enterprise shall not be deemed to have a permanent establishment in a contracting state merely because it carries on business in that state through a broker, general commission agent or any other agent of an independent status, provided that such persons are acting in the ordinary course of their business.

In principle this provision should allow a company to develop a sales or distribution network in other jurisdictions without attracting a tax liability in the jurisdiction(s) in question. However, where the creation of a sales network involves the use of dependent agents these are likely to be regarded as representing permanent establishments and, as a consequence, would result in a liability to tax in the jurisdiction in which they are based. By locating the sales company in a jurisdiction which is close to its markets, this would allow the company to exercise a high degree of supervision over an independent sales force and so put off the need to appoint a dependent sales team which would give rise to such tax liabilities.

For this reason, sales companies are frequently based in Switzerland (for the European markets), Cyprus (for Middle Eastern markets) and Hong Kong or Singapore (for the Far Eastern markets). Hong Kong does not benefit from any double tax agreements, although offshore profits are not subject to tax in Hong Kong. Singapore has an extensive network of double tax agreements but has a relatively high rate of corporation tax.

As any sales company is likely to be subject to attack under either transfer pricing legislation or controlled foreign company/Sub-Chapter F legislation, it is essential to be able to demonstrate its involvement in the creation of a sales or distribution network in order to substantiate that it fulfils a real economic function.

Purchasing/buying companies

Where a specific region is the source of considerable quantities of product for a trading company, for example a store group, it often makes commercial sense to set up a purchasing or buying company in that region. This company may take over responsibility for identifying new products and suppliers, negotiating terms and undertaking quality controls before arranging shipment of the goods.

Although such a company would operate as a profit centre in its own right, the revenue authorities are likely to take a close interest in its level of profits and the same anti-avoidance legislation would be relevant as could in principle be applied to a sales company.

Examples of such purchasing companies are those which have been established in Hong Kong by some of the major retailers to obtain electronic consumer products and textiles from the region.

Overseas employment companies

In addition to granting tax concessions to foreign nationals or other categories of 'voluntary' residents, some jurisdictions offer tax concessions to their own residents where they are employed by an overseas company and perform the duties of their employment overseas. In order to take advantage of these concessions, a number of multinationals have formed overseas employment companies which employ both overseas personnel and local staff who undertake duties outside the jurisdiction in which they are resident.

10
Holding Companies and Co-ordination Centres

Location of a parent company

Just as an individual's nationality is an accident of birth, so the country of residence of the ultimate parent company of a multinational is often simply the country of its original inception. A group will expand and develop from an essentially domestic base, to which the social and cultural ties of the head office management will continue to bind the group even although its overseas activities may well have outgrown it. Anti-avoidance legislation or other regulatory controls such as exchange controls, which prevent a company from transferring its residence abroad, may serve as an additional anchor, securing it to its country of origin, as may the presence of an exit or toll charge which causes all capital gains to crystallise when a company migrates.

For this reason, the country of residence of a parent company is rarely considered as a variable when reviewing the tax strategy of a group. Where a significant disadvantage results from the tax regime of the parent company, the group may well become the target of a takeover by a company based in a country with a more favourable tax regime.

The use of an intermediate holding company

It may be beneficial, for a number of reasons, for a group to own overseas investments through an intermediate holding company (ie, a company based outside the country of residence of both the ultimate parent company and the country of residence of the underlying investment). Apart from the general commercial advantage that the country chosen as a location for such a company may provide a more favourable climate than the ultimate home country so far as concerns exchange control and other regulatory requirements affecting overseas investment, there may be specific tax advantages associated with the use of an intermediate holding company. The possible advantages are as follows.

Reducing withholding taxes suffered
The country of residence of the intermediate holding company may have negotiated a more favourable network of double tax agreements than the ultimate home country and this may result in the intermediate holding

company suffering a lower level of withholding tax in respect of dividends received. Provided that the country of residence of the intermediate holding company does not levy a withholding tax on the payment of dividends or impose other taxes which either exceed or claw back the savings made in respect of dividends received, this will result in an overall reduction in tax.

Deferring tax arising on gains realised on the eventual disposal of investments

Ideally the country in which an intermediate holding company is resident should not tax capital gains arising on the disposal of investments. Such a charge would act as a toll or exit charge and would restrict severely a group's ability to restructure in the future if, for any reason, it wished to own the investments either directly or through an alternative jurisdiction. Whereas the Netherlands does not levy any tax on such gains, Switzerland does and this has led to a decline in its use as a holding company location.

As the majority of capital exporting countries tax gains arising on the disposal of investments, the use of an intermediate holding company based in a country such as the Netherlands will enable the tax charge which would have arisen in the home country to be deferred. This would be the case only where the home country's anti-avoidance legislation does not tax such gains. The UK's controlled foreign company legislation taxes income which accrues to certain categories of overseas company, but not capital gains.

Deferring tax in respect of overseas income

Where the country of residence of the parent company operates a system of worldwide taxation, the use of an intermediate holding company may enable the parent company to defer tax in its home country by not remitting dividends received. Thus an intermediate holding company may serve as a dividend trap which reinvests its income, instead of remitting it to the parent company. Clearly it is essential that the country in which the intermediate holding company is based does not itself tax such income.

The majority of capital exporting countries have anti-avoidance legislation aimed at preventing the abuse of the deferral which is at the heart of most systems of worldwide taxation. This deferral allows the profits of an overseas resident operating company to be taxed only when remitted by way of a dividend. The attempt to delay further the point at which the profits of overseas operating companies fall into charge to tax in the home country, by using an intermediate holding company as a dividend trap, has resulted in the introduction of anti-avoidance legislation along the lines of the US Sub-Part F legislation and the UK's controlled foreign company legislation. However, even where anti-avoidance legislation of this kind is in place, it may still be possible (as in the UK) to obtain the benefit of a deferral even although this may be substantially reduced.

Maximising credit for foreign taxes

Any system of worldwide taxation will have its own conventions for matching dividend income with the underlying profits of the overseas companies and for attributing the overseas tax suffered to these profits. Inevitably these conventions will give rise to anomalies and will introduce considerable complexities into the administration of the tax function. Accordingly, it is essential to ensure that the underlying tax is calculated on a regular basis, and not just when a dividend is remitted or the underlying profits otherwise fall into charge to tax in the home country. Although this may seem obvious good practice, the majority of UK groups, unlike US multinationals, do not follow it.

Under certain conventions for giving relief for foreign taxes, overseas income from a variety of sources may be pooled, so as to average the underlying rate of tax. However, even where such a pooling of overseas income is not permitted under domestic legislation, it may be possible to achieve it by routing the various overseas sources of income through an intermediate holding company. Depending on the legislation in the jurisdiction of the ultimate parent company, this may have the effect of converting overseas income from a variety of sources into overseas income from a single, overseas source, ie the jurisdiction of the intermediate holding company.

The benefits of being able to pool various sources of overseas income for the purpose of averaging the underlying rates of tax are illustrated in Examples I to III. Example I shows how unrelieved overseas tax arises where a UK resident company receives dividends from a country with a higher rate of tax.

Example I

		Overseas tax suffered
Net dividend received	105,000	
Withholding tax (30%)	45,000	45,000
	150,000	
Underlying tax suffered	60,000	60,000
UK taxable income	£210,000	£105,000
Corporation tax thereon		
33% of £210,000	69,300	
Double tax relief	(69,300)	(69,300)
Unrelieved overseas tax		£35,700

Example II shows how additional tax is payable where the same company receives a dividend from a country with a lower rate of tax than the UK.

Example II

		Overseas tax suffered
Dividend received	100,000	
Underlying tax suffered	10,000	10,000
UK taxable income	£110,000	
Corporation tax at 33%	36,300	
Less: double tax relief	(10,000)	(10,000)
UK residual liability	£26,300	–

Accordingly where a company has investments in both countries, generating profits and incurring tax as shown in Examples I and II, it will suffer an overall tax burden of £105,000 + £36,300 (including £26,300 of UK residual tax) = £141,300 in total. Where, on the other hand, the company pools or averages the overseas tax liabilities through an intermediate holding company based in a country which imposes no tax on profits which pass through it, this will result in a saving of the UK (residual) liability. This is illustrated in Example III.

Example III

Dividend (grossed up: £210,000 + £110,000)	£320,000
Corporation tax thereon at 33%	105,600
Less: double tax relief (£105,000 + £10,000)	(115,000)
Unrelieved overseas tax	£(9,400)

Instead of suffering unrelieved overseas tax of £35,700 as in Example I, this has been reduced by the residual UK liability of £26,300, suffered in Example II. Thus where overseas income is pooled or averaged in this way the total tax incurred is reduced to £115,000, instead of the combined tax charge of £141,300 from Examples I and II.

Characteristics of an ideal holding company

The principal characteristics of an ideal holding company location are:

(1) the absence of tax on dividend or other income;
(2) the existence of a favourable network of double tax agreements which limit withholding taxes levied on the payment of dividends by host countries;
(3) the ability to remit dividends to the ultimate home country without incurring any, or only a reduced rate of, withholding tax;
(4) the absence of tax on any profit arising on the disposal of an investment;
(5) the absence of tax on capital introduced to a company or on increases in a company's share capital.

However, a country which imposes little or no tax will not be in a position to negotiate a favourable network of double tax agreements and, as a consequence, it will usually be necessary to combine two jurisdictions in order to achieve the optimum structure.

The following are the most frequently used locations for intermediate holding companies.

Netherlands

The Netherlands has an extensive and favourable network of double tax agreements, which reduces or eliminates withholding taxes on dividends paid to a company which is resident there. In addition, under the terms of the majority of double tax agreements into which the Netherlands has entered, a reduced rate of withholding tax applies where dividends are paid by a Dutch company to a company which is resident in a treaty partner country; often this rate is reduced to 5 per cent. Where the ultimate parent company is resident within a member state of the European Community and certain other conditions are satisfied (see Chapter 11: *The Netherlands and Netherlands Antilles in International Tax Planning*, pages 144–145), no withholding tax is payable when a dividend is paid. Where a withholding tax applies to a dividend which is remitted to the ultimate parent company, this will need to be taken into account in evaluating the costs/benefits of this structure. For example, it was still attractive to the majority of UK multinationals to use a Dutch intermediate holding company when a 5 per cent withholding tax applied to dividends paid to the UK parent. Reworking Example III on the basis of a 5 per cent rate of withholding tax would give the situation shown in Example IV.

Example IV

Gross dividends (£210,000 + £110,000)		£320,000
Dutch withholding tax (5% × £105,000 + £100,000)	10,250	
Other overseas taxes suffered (per Example III)	115,000	
Revised overseas tax suffered	£125,250	
UK corporation tax at 33% on £320,000	105,600	
Less double tax relief	125,250	
Unrelieved overseas tax	£19,650	

Thus the overall tax saving in Example III of £26,300 has been reduced by £10,250 (the additional withholding tax suffered). However, the use of an intermediate holding company, in Example IV, would still generate tax savings of £16,050 (ignoring compliance costs associated with the structure).

Where the ultimate parent company has no unrelieved overseas taxes, the tax costs arising in the intermediate jurisdiction may be fully relievable. In this case, these costs will be borne entirely by the exchequer of the home country, with the taxpayer benefiting in full from the tax savings arising from his ability to average the underlying rates of tax.

An additional advantage enjoyed by the Netherlands as a location for a holding company is that it is not essential for the ultimate parent company to be resident in a country which has entered into a double tax agreement with the Netherlands for a reduced rate of withholding tax to apply to dividends paid to it. This is because a Dutch company may pay a dividend to a parent company in the Netherlands Antilles and be required to withhold tax of only either 7½ or 5 per cent under the terms of the so-called Kingdom agreement. The higher 7½ per cent rate applies where the income of the Netherlands Antilles parent company is subject to a preferential tax regime under which dividend income is taxed at between 2.4 and 3 per cent and exempt from the so-called island surcharge. In practice, the majority of Antilles parent companies have opted to be taxed at a higher rate than this minimum rate, in order to benefit from the lower 5 per cent rate of withholding tax in respect of dividends paid by a Dutch intermediate holding company. At the same time they have used a number of techniques to reduce the effective rate of tax suffered in the Antilles and so minimise the overall tax costs involved in the structure.

Dividends received by a Dutch company will be exempt from tax in the Netherlands provided that the participation exemption applies. The participation exemption will apply where:

(1) both the share owning and the shareholding companies are active investments. Whereas a portfolio investment involves the passive investment of surplus cash, an active investment will involve economic integration within the context of a wider group, with the parent company undertaking a proactive supervisory role. (However, this provision does not apply where the shareholding exceeds 25 per cent and represents an investment in another member state of the EC.)
(2) the shareholding is at least 5 per cent of the paid-up capital of the underlying company;
(3) the underlying company is subject to tax on its profits at a national level.

In addition, capital gains arising from the disposal of an investment which benefits from the participation exemption are exempt from tax. The absence of tax in respect of such capital gains is essential if, because of a change in the tax laws in the home country of the ultimate parent company, or for some other reason, it becomes necessary to restructure the group or to dismantle the structure.

(See Chapter 11: *The Netherlands and Netherlands Antilles in International Tax Planning* for a fuller description.)

Switzerland

Switzerland used to be a favoured location in which to locate intermediate holding companies. However, it has a number of inherent disadvantages, which have discouraged its use in recent years; the principal being that it taxes gains arising from the disposal of investments. Those groups which have a Swiss intermediate holding company in their structure are often locked in by the capital gains tax liabilities which would arise out of any attempt to restructure their investments.

Switzerland imposes tax at three levels: the federal, the cantonal and the communal. Most pure holding companies can obtain exemption from cantonal and communal taxes and will be subject to cantonal net worth taxes only at reduced rates. Federal taxation is progressive and applies at varying rates up to a maximum of 9.8 per cent. Where the dividend income arises from a shareholding which represents at least 20 per cent of the paying company's share capital or has a value of not less than SFr 2 million, the dividend income will be eligible for a form of participation exemption. Unlike the Dutch participation exemption which exempts eligible income from tax, the Swiss participation relief is by way of a reduction in income tax otherwise payable and is calculated as a percentage of eligible income to other income. This calculation is illustrated in Example V.

Example V

Dividend income	
(net of irrecoverable withholding tax)	SFr 800.00
Interest income	80.00
Less expenses	(200.00)
Profit	680.00
Federal tax thereon	
(assume maximum rate) 9.8%	66.60
Less relief for dividends	
$\frac{800}{880} \times 100 = 91\% \times 66.6$	(60.60)
Tax payable	SFr 6.00

(Because of the way in which the relief is calculated, full relief is only available where the dividend income equals the total gross income.)

Another disadvantage associated with the use of Switzerland is the incorporation into its domestic legislation of the anti-treaty abuse decree of 1962. This contains the requirement that a company must distribute each year at least 25 per cent of its treaty protected income as a dividend which is subject to Swiss withholding taxes. Unlike the Netherlands with its agreement with the Netherlands Antilles, Switzerland has not entered into any double tax agreements with tax havens which would allow income to be distributed out of Switzerland at a low tax cost. As a consequence, the country in which the ultimate parent company is resident must have a favourable double tax agreement with Switzerland which either eliminates or substantially reduces the 35 per cent rate of withholding tax which applies where dividends are paid by a Swiss company to a company resident in a non-treaty country.

A further disadvantage of Switzerland as a location for a holding company is the 3 per cent tax payable on capital contributed on the formation of a company or on the increase in a company's share capital. This compares with the 1 per cent levied in the Netherlands.

Luxembourg

Under the law of 1929 a Luxembourg holding company is a company whose sole object is the ownership and administration of shares. As such, it is exempt from direct taxation in Luxembourg and is only subject to two levies:

(1) capital levy at the rate of 1 per cent of the value of capital contributed to the company by the shareholders;
(2) an annual tax at the rate of 0.2 per cent, based on the aggregate value of the issued shares.

Apart from the prohibition on a holding company engaging in any direct commercial undertaking, this type of holding company suffers from a serious disadvantage in that it is specifically excluded from the benefit of all double tax agreements into which Luxembourg has entered. Accordingly, all dividends paid to such a company will be subject to the maximum rate of withholding tax applicable in the host country.

In order to overcome these two problems, Luxembourg amended its tax legislation in 1990 to enable a Luxembourg company to obtain the benefit of a participation exemption, regardless of whether or not it operates exclusively as a holding company. This participation exemption has the effect of exempting dividend income from tax where:

(1) the dividend paying company is resident in Luxembourg and fully liable to tax or if not resident in Luxembourg is subject to tax at a rate of at least 15 per cent;
(2) the shareholder owns at least 10 per cent of the share capital or the initial value of the investment is a minimum of Lux Frs 50 million;
(3) the shares have been held for at least 12 months prior to the payment of a dividend.

In addition to the exemption of dividend income from corporate tax, the shares will be exempt from capital gains tax provided that the company owns at least 25 per cent of the share capital. However, although capital gains are exempt from tax, capital losses will be deductible, whether realised or unrealised.

Expenses in excess of exempt income are tax deductible and foreign withholding taxes are creditable (subject to the general principles of the tax legislation). In order to benefit from these provisions, a company would clearly need other, non-exempt income. Losses are available for indefinite carry forward.

Capital taxes – net worth tax of 0.5 per cent and municipal business tax of approximately the same rate – will not apply if the underlying company is newly formed during the period or the shares are acquired in the calendar year when the Luxembourg company was formed; otherwise the exemption is not available during the first year of ownership.

Although a withholding tax of 15 per cent may apply to dividend payments by a Luxembourg holding company, this is reduced under the terms of most double tax agreements to between 5 and 2.5 per cent.

A problem associated with the use of this new style of holding company is the uncertainty as to whether treaty partners will accept that the benefit of existing agreements may apply to such companies.

Other locations

A number of other countries have tried to establish themselves as possible locations for intermediate holding companies. However, the attractions of the Netherlands remain overwhelming although even these are being rapidly eroded by the development of anti-avoidance legislation. Austria and Cyprus both advertised their network of double tax agreements with Eastern Europe as a principal attraction; recent developments in Eastern Europe have reduced the value of this in the eyes of potential investors. Other countries, such as Ireland and France, have a tax on capital gains which limits their attractions. France introduced legislation to remove the tax trap that imputation systems put across the path of investors who are in receipt of overseas income (see Chapter 2: *Tax Systems and their Interaction*, pages 24–26 for further details) but did not address the issue of the tax charge on capital gains. The UK has addressed neither the problem posed by its imputation system nor its tax on capital gains.

Remitting profits to the home country

Where the home country of the ultimate parent company applies an exemption system, the emphasis of tax planning will be on saving tax in the host country. Where, for any reason, overseas income does not benefit from the exemption, the emphasis of tax planning will on converting it into tax exempt dividend income by routing it through some other jurisdiction.

On the other hand, where a system of worldwide taxation applies, tax planning will be more complex. This is because the emphasis will not only be on minimising tax in the host country but also on maximising the double tax relief or foreign tax credits. The calculation of foreign tax credits/double tax relief will be governed by detailed provisions in the domestic tax legislation of the home country. It is difficult to generalise about these rules; they will either:

(1) permit the pooling of profits for the purpose of calculating the underlying tax where these originate from a variety of jurisdictions (thus indirectly subsidising high tax jurisdictions);
(2) permit the pooling of profits (usually by default) where these are routed through an intermediate holding company;
(3) apply a country by country restriction;
(4) apply an even more restrictive source by source rule, as in the UK. Although in the case of the UK, (2) above applies where a group routes income through an intermediate holding company.

In addition to these conventions, there will also be conventions for attributing the foreign tax to the income. For example, the tax legislation of the home country may deem income from overseas subsidiaries to have been distributed on first-in first out, last-in last-out, or on some other basis, such as by reference to the commercial law of the host country. Where the host country taxes profits on a preceding year basis (Hong Kong) or some other average basis (Switzerland), the home country will need a convention to define whether the overseas tax charge is matched with the income of the period when it arose, or the income of the period when the tax liability arises. Where a restrictive source by source attribution of foreign tax credits applies, there will be conventions to attribute those tax liabilities which arise in host countries which permit some form of group relief or consolidated filing.

Whatever conventions the home country adopts, it is essential to maintain ongoing records matching the underlying tax with the relevant income in order to maximise relief. It should be borne in mind that a saving of double tax relief/foreign tax credit has a £ for £ or $ for $ value, whereas additional profits are worth only 65p in the £ or 65 cents in the $ in a jurisdiction which taxes profits at the rate of 35 per cent. The presence of excess double tax relief/foreign tax credits in a group which is tax-paying, may be indicative of inefficiencies in tax planning.

In addition to seeking to maximise double tax relief/foreign tax credits, a group based in a country operating a system of worldwide taxation will try to repatriate overseas income in a tax-free form. Depending on the jurisdiction involved, it may be possible to achieve this by arranging for a subsidiary company to waive a loan or to make a gift either directly to the parent company or to a fellow subsidiary company based in the same jurisdiction (on the basis that it may be harder for the revenue authorities to recharacterise the payment as a dividend where it does not flow directly to the parent company). Alternatively, it may be possible to import the residence of a non-resident company into the country of residence of the ultimate parent company, provided that this importation does not trigger a tax liability. Once resident, it may be possible to make a tax-free distribution of the company's retained reserves at the date of importation, on the basis that inter-group dividends are tax-free where both the payer and recipient are resident companies.

Where there is no immediate requirement to remit profits to the home country because the parent company has sufficient reserves or domestic income out of which to service dividend payments, a tax deferral may be obtained by arranging for subsidiaries in low tax jurisdictions to lend surplus funds either to the parent company or another company in the domestic group. However, in the US upstream loans of this kind are treated as dividends. Although the UK proposed, in 1981, introducing anti-avoidance legislation to attack this practice, a policy decision was taken not to proceed with the legislation because of the substantial one-off cash flow cost to business (in respect of pre-existing upstream loans). The introduction of the controlled foreign company legislation has limited, in any event, the tax deferral arising from the deduction in the UK of interest arising on the loan and the accrual of the corresponding interest income in a tax haven. It was further considered likely that commercial requirements would necessitate the ultimate distribution of profits to the parent company or domestic group (at which time they would fall into charge to tax in any event).

Anti-avoidance and intermediate holding companies

Apart from regulatory controls which may restrict a parent company's ability to set up an intermediate holding company, there is a rapidly developing body of anti-avoidance legislation which will affect its operation. As a pure holding company is likely to involve only limited substantive activity, the first hurdle will be to satisfy the relevant revenue authorities that it is indeed effectively managed, or managed and controlled, in the chosen jurisdiction. Where the intermediate holding company also acts as a co-ordination centre, or performs other administrative functions, from a base within its chosen location, this will help to substantiate that it is indeed resident there.

Controlled foreign company or sub Part F type legislation may prevent income which accrues to a passive (ie non-operating) company from escaping tax in the ultimate home country. It may achieve this by, for example, deeming the income to have been remitted to the parent company. The majority of developed countries now have anti-avoidance legislation of this kind on their statute books.

Where an intermediate holding company is being superimposed on operating companies and savings in withholding taxes result from this, the jurisdictions in which the operating companies are based may be able to set aside the structure by applying a general anti-avoidance doctrine. Examples of such doctrines are the Swiss and Dutch concept of 'fraus legis' or the French concept of 'abus de droit' which enable the respective tax authorities to set aside artificial transactions whose purpose is to undermine the intent of the legislation. In addition to such doctrines, there may be general anti-conduit rulings which would prevent treaty shopping in this way. However, certain double tax agreements contain specific limitations on the availability of particular benefits limiting them to 'bona fide' residents of the treaty partner country. For example, certain double tax agreements into which the UK has entered provide for a refund to an overseas shareholder of a proportion of the tax credit imputed to domestic shareholders; this particular benefit invariably is restricted to bona fide residents of the treaty partner country. The US is insisting on the inclusion of a general limitation of benefit provision in any double tax agreement which it either negotiates or renegotiates.

Co-ordination centres

Where a multinational group has significant interests in a region which is distant from its head office, it is often desirable to set up a regional headquarter or co-ordination centre to oversee and co-ordinate its various business interests in the particular region. Such centres will usually provide the full range of administrative and management functions associated with a head office; for example, treasury and tax management, internal audit, public relations, market research and marketing, insurance and accounting.

Where a multinational holds overseas investments through an intermediate holding company, it makes good commercial sense to arrange for any regional co-ordination function to be undertaken by that company as this will lend substance and help demonstrate that it is indeed resident in that country. However, although a multinational may own its overseas investments through an intermediate holding company, where it operates in a number of regions it is likely to require more than one regional co-ordination centre and it may be considered commercially undesirable to have a regional co-ordination centre in the Far East which is a branch of a Dutch company, for example. Other multinationals may own their overseas investments directly because the tax advantages associated with indirect ownership are either not available to them or are not relevant to their circumstances. Such multinationals are likely to require nevertheless to co-ordinate the activities of their subsidiaries in various regions.

Although the majority of countries which are attractive locations for intermediate holding companies provide a suitable tax environment for a co-ordination centre, a far wider range of countries are attractive locations for co-ordination centres. (However, Switzerland and Luxembourg both suffer from a significant commercial disadvantage for such operations, namely a relative shortage of skilled labour.) The UK, which is ruled out as a location for a holding company because of the advance corporation tax which foreign dividends attract and also because of its tax on capital gains, can be an attractive location for such operations. The UK revenue authorities accept that an essentially administrative function does not constitute a trading activity and as such is not taxable (where the nature of its activity is not so clearly non-taxable, it is possible to agree to be taxed on a percentage mark-up of expenses). There is also the additional advantage of a relatively low overall burden of tax on foreign nationals who may be involved in the business of the co-ordination centre. As staff costs are usually a sizeable proportion of the overall cost structure of such an operation, a number of other countries have special tax regimes which apply to expatriate staff. The Netherlands, France and Belgium all have special regimes for both tax and social security purposes for this category of staff.

So far as concerns the general tax principles applicable to co-ordination centre activities, under the domestic tax legislation of a number of countries an essentially administrative activity which does not involve the negotiation and conclusion of sales contracts will not give rise to a tax liability in any event. This position is supported by the OECD Model Double Tax Convention, which states that a permanent establishment (which brings an activity within the taxing jurisdiction of another state) shall be deemed not to include the maintenance of a fixed place of business solely for the purpose of purchasing goods or merchandise or of collecting information for the enterprise or the maintenance of a fixed place of business solely for the purpose of carrying on, for the enterprise, any other activity of a preparatory or auxiliary nature.

Belgian co-ordination centres

Where a country had concluded a double tax agreement with Belgium, a company which was resident in the treaty partner country would not be subject to tax in Belgium in respect of any office, which it set up to provide essentially administrative services, there. This simply follows the principle set out in the OECD Model Double Tax Convention. However, this rule only applied where Belgium had concluded a double tax agreement with the relevant country. In 1982 the Belgian Government not only extended the definition of services which such a centre could provide but also allowed companies based in countries with which Belgium had not entered into a double tax treaty, as well as Belgian subsidiary companies, to benefit from the co-ordination centre provisions where the following requirements are satisfied.

(1) It must be part of an international group with at least Bfr 500 million or 20 per cent of its consolidated capital and reserves abroad.
(2) It must generate a total consolidated turnover outside Belgium of at least Bfr 5 billion or 20 per cent of its total.
(3) It must have at least four overseas subsidiaries, in different countries, based outside the country of residence of the parent company. These subsidiaries must have been owned for at least two years before applying for co-ordination centre status.
(4) Within two years of commencing its activities, the co-ordination centre must employ at least ten full-time staff in Belgium. (These may be foreign employees in which case they are exempt from work permit requirements. In addition, they may benefit from a special tax regime.)

Financial institutions may not benefit from the co-ordination centre provisions.

Tax treatment of Belgian co-ordination centres

A co-ordination centre is subject to corporate tax on the basis of a percentage of its overhead expenses (excluding personnel costs and financial charges). This percentage is subject to agreement with the Belgian revenue authorities and its precise level depends on the mark-up the co-ordination centre itself applies to the expenditure which it recharges to its affiliated companies. However, its taxable income may not fall below:

(1) its disallowed expenses; and
(2) benefits which are in excess of those which would have been realised when dealing at arm's length.

In addition, co-ordination centres are exempt from withholding tax in respect of dividends, interest and royalty payments. They are also exempt from registration tax in respect of capital contributions.

In certain circumstances, interest received by a Belgian co-ordination centre will be treated as having a deemed withholding tax attaching to it which may be creditable against an actual tax liability or refundable. Likewise, there are circumstances when a dividend paid by a Belgian co-ordination centre to another Belgian company will be treated as having a deemed withholding tax attaching to it.

Certain older established co-ordination centres can continue to benefit from the above tax benefits into the foreseeable future. However, co-ordination centres set up more recently may only enjoy the above tax benefits for a ten-year period.

Possible uses of a Belgian co-ordination centre

A co-ordination centre may be particularly advantageous as a group financing vehicle, especially as a reinvoicing company for the purpose of managing a group's currency exposure. In addition, it may be used as a means of financing group companies by factoring debts owing to operating companies.

Hong Kong and Singapore

Both Hong Kong and Singapore have developed infrastructures, including excellent communication and transport links not only with the Asia Pacific region but also with the rest of the world. In 1986 Singapore introduced special tax incentives for so-called operational headquarter companies (OHQs) or co-ordination centres. Under these incentives, a reduced rate of tax of 10 per cent applies to headquarter-related income; management fees, royalty and interest income are the most obvious examples. In order to obtain approved status and so benefit from these incentives, a branch or company must satisfy criteria relating to minimum capital, turnover, number of employees, and range of services as well as the number of companies to which it provides those services. Clearly these tax incentives are only relevant where the OHQ is a profit centre, as opposed to a mere cost centre. In the case of management fees, it is sometimes undesirable to charge out management fees with a mark-up because this may result in the whole payment becoming subject to withholding tax; in some countries, such as Malaysia, withholding tax is not applied to a payment which is shown to be a simple recharge of expenses incurred. Dividend income received by such companies is also exempt from Singapore tax for a predetermined period and may be paid to shareholders without attracting any tax.

Unlike Singapore, Hong Kong does not have a network of double tax agreements. It levies tax at the rate of 16 per cent but only in respect of Hong Kong source profits. The precise definition of Hong Kong source profits is the subject of considerable uncertainty, especially in the case of categories of income such as management fees which may involve activities in both Hong Kong and the country of source.

Both Hong Kong and Singapore have favourable tax regimes for employees, especially where part of their duties is performed outside the respective territory.

11
The Netherlands and Netherlands Antilles in International Tax Planning

The Netherlands

The importance of the Netherlands in international tax planning lies in the fact that it combines an extensive and generally favourable network of double tax agreements (see Appendix III) with a domestic tax regime which has a number of advantageous features, especially in relation to outward investment.

The Netherlands cannot be regarded as a tax haven as it taxes corporate profits at between 35 and 40 per cent and imposes a withholding tax of 25 per cent on dividend payments to a non-treaty country. These relatively high rates of tax have enabled the Netherlands to negotiate a network of double tax agreements. However, despite not being a tax haven, the Dutch tax regime has a number of especially advantageous features. In particular, it does not tax either dividend income or capital gains arising from the disposal of investments where these benefit from the so-called participation exemption nor does it tax the profits of an overseas branch where certain conditions are met (see branch exemption, page 147). Furthermore, no withholding tax is imposed under its domestic tax legislation on payments of royalties and interest (except in respect of certain profit-sharing bonds). This enables these to be received in the Netherlands under the protection of the relevant double tax agreement and then paid out to a low tax jurisdiction, without attracting withholding tax. However, not all of a company's income may be paid out in a tax deductible form as the arm's length principle requires a margin of profit to be left in any intermediate company. The administrative practice, adopted by the Dutch revenue authorities, of giving advance rulings in certain circumstances, enables this margin of profit to be agreed in advance with the result that taxpayers can enter into transactions secure in the knowledge of their tax consequences (in the Netherlands, at least).

Under the terms of a number of double tax agreements, the Netherlands reduces the rate of withholding tax on the payment of dividends to 5 per cent where the recipient company owns 25 per cent or more of the share capital of the Dutch company. Where the Dutch subsidiary's parent company is based in Switzerland or a member state of the European Community, this withholding tax may be eliminated altogether. Because dividend income can flow into the Netherlands, protected from high rates of withholding tax by its network of double tax agreements and without incurring a tax liability in the Netherlands by virtue of the participation exemption, the Netherlands may be an attractive location in which to base an intermediate holding company. The profits of this company may then flow out to the ultimate parent company with a reduced or nil rate of withholding tax.

The benefits of using an intermediate holding company include (these are discussed at greater length in Chapter 10: *Holding Companies and Co-ordination Centres* – pages 126–128):

(1) reducing the level of withholding tax suffered on dividend income – this will apply where the double tax agreement between the Netherlands and the host country is more favourable than the agreement between the host country and the country of residence of the ultimate parent company;
(2) maximising credit for foreign taxes; by pooling these through an intermediate holding company;
(3) deferring tax in respect of any capital gain arising on the disposal of investments. As the Netherlands does not charge tax on such gains and provided that the country of residence of the ultimate holding company does not have anti-avoidance legislation intended to bring these into immediate charge to tax, a liability will only arise either when the profit is remitted or when the intermediate holding company is itself liquidated or disposed of;
(4) deferring tax which would otherwise arise on the direct remittance of dividends to the country of residence of the ultimate parent company. By receiving dividends through a Dutch intermediate holding company which reinvests its profits outside the Netherlands, no Dutch tax liability would arise and the tax liability in the home country would be deferred, in the absence of anti-avoidance legislation aimed at controlled foreign companies.

Although dividend income which benefits from the participation exemption is not subject to tax in the Netherlands, other income is liable to tax at a rate of 35 or 40 per cent. Accordingly, the Netherlands is an unattractive jurisdiction in which to retain profits. Profits which flow into the Netherlands should consequently be reinvested outside the Netherlands or paid out by way of dividends, royalties or interest. This reinvestment may either take the form of new or additional investments which qualify for the participation exemption or be in overseas activities which will qualify for the branch exemption. In both of these cases, future income from such investments will benefit from exemption from tax in the Netherlands.

The Netherlands and Netherlands Antilles

Even where the ultimate parent company of a multinational is based in a country which does not have a double tax agreement with the Netherlands, the 25 per cent rate of Dutch withholding tax, which would apply to the payment of dividends in such circumstances, can be reduced. This can be achieved by owning the shares in the Dutch company through a company based in the Netherlands Antilles; in which case a withholding tax of 5 or 7½ per cent will apply. This particularly favourable rate of withholding tax is granted under the terms of the so-called Kingdom agreement and can be explained by the constitutional relationship of the Netherlands and Netherlands Antilles.

The Netherlands together with the Netherlands Antilles and Aruba comprise the Kingdom of the Netherlands. The Netherlands Antilles and Aruba are situated in the Caribbean, off the coast of Venezuela and Puerto Rico. Although Aruba originally formed part of the Netherlands Antilles, after 1986 it became a separate country within the Kingdom of the Netherlands. Since this time it has pursued its own independent fiscal policy of developing as a traditional Caribbean tax haven. The Netherlands Antilles, however, has retained the fiscal advantage of the reduced rate of withholding tax applicable to dividend payments by Dutch subsidiaries to their Antilles parent companies and granted under the terms of the Kingdom agreement. Until 1986, no withholding tax at all was levied on dividend payments from Dutch subsidiaries to the Netherlands Antilles. However, in response to international pressure, particularly from the US, the Netherlands was forced to revise its agreement with the Netherlands Antilles and introduce a two-tier rate of withholding tax: 5 or 7½ per cent.

The reduced 5 per cent rate applies where the profits of the Netherlands Antilles company are subject to profits tax of at least 5½ per cent in the Netherlands Antilles, otherwise the higher 7½ per cent rate will apply. This latter rate will apply where the Netherlands Antilles company is subject to a special incentive regime under which profits are taxed at the reduced rate of between 2.4 and 3 per cent, and no so-called island surcharge is imposed.

Special incentive regimes also apply to the taxation of finance companies, licensing companies, insurance companies, overseas real estate companies and a variety of other categories of company. The special incentive rate of tax of 2.4 to 3 per cent compares with an ordinary rate of tax (inclusive of island surcharge) of between 31.5 and 39.1 per cent. No withholding tax applies to the payment of dividends by a Netherlands Antilles company and gains arising from the disposal of investments are also exempt from tax.

It is usual for holding companies to opt to be taxed in the Netherlands Antilles at a higher rate than the special incentive rate of 2.4 to 3 per cent in order to obtain the benefit of the reduced rate of Dutch withholding tax of 5 per cent. At the same time, the overall level of dividends payable by the Dutch company can be reduced by the use of gearing, thus extracting profits in the form of interest payments. A variety of tax planning techniques are used to reduce the effective rate of tax in the Netherlands Antilles. However, the Dutch revenue authorities are understood to be putting increasing pressure on the Netherlands Antilles authorities to curb these practices. In addition, they are also understood to be seeking to revise upwards the rate(s) of withholding tax on dividend payments to the Netherlands Antilles.

The participation exemption in the Netherlands

The participation exemption was originally introduced in order to avoid the double taxation of dividends which would otherwise arise where dividends flow between companies. The participation exemption overcomes this by exempting dividends from tax in the hands of the recipient company. Although the exemption originally applied only to dividends from shares in another resident company, it was soon extended to include dividends received from non-resident companies. Later, it was extended further to exclude from tax any gain arising on the disposal of such shares.

As the income from an investment which benefits from the participation exemption is exempt from tax, by the same token associated expenses are non-deductible. Such expenses include interest, currency losses and professional fees. Borrowings incurred within six months of making an acquisition are deemed to have been incurred for the purpose of the acquisition and related interest expenses are disallowed as a consequence.

Even although a gain arising from an investment benefiting from the participation exemption is not subject to tax, a loss resulting from the liquidation of such an investment may qualify for relief. However, this relief applies only where the investment is liquidated and not if it is sold. In addition, there are detailed anti-avoidance provisions which restrict the right to a deduction where the loss, or part of it, is attributable to a loan account which has been converted subsequently into capital or where the loss arises from an investment which has been transferred into the Netherlands with a view to realising the loss.

Because of the importance of the participation exemption in international tax planning, practitioners need to understand, if only in outline, the requirements which have to be met for an investment to qualify.

(1) The Dutch parent company must own at least 5 per cent of the paid-up share capital of the distributing company. Where an investment is substantial but nevertheless falls below the 5 per cent limit, an

exception to this requirement may be made but, in these circumstances, an advance ruling should be obtained. In the case of an investment in another member state of the EC, the participation exemption will still apply if, instead of owning 5 per cent of the paid-up share capital, the Dutch parent owns 25 per cent of the voting rights in the company and the double tax agreement between the Netherlands and the member state in question grants a reduction in the rate of withholding tax on dividends by reference to voting rights.

The participation exemption will not apply to shareholdings which are held for trading purposes, ie with a view to resale.

(2) Neither the Dutch holding company nor the investment (in the case of a non-EC investment) should represent a passive or portfolio investment, ie one which is held solely for the purpose of generating a return on the investment.

The question of whether a holding or intermediate holding company represents a passive investment has been the subject of some controversy. Following a decision of the Supreme Court in 1973, the Under Minister of Finance issued a statement to clarify the matter. This statement indicates that the status of an intermediate holding company will be determined largely by reference to the function of the ultimate holding company. Where this performs clearly defined management functions in relation to its subsidiaries, and as such fulfils an active role, the intermediate holding company will be regarded in the same light.

The underlying investment must be an actual operating company. Although the Dutch Revenue authorities gave, in August 1988, an advance ruling under which they confirmed that the participation exemption would apply to a 20 per cent shareholding in a Luxembourg holding company whose only investment was in an operating company, recently this ruling was withdrawn.

(3) Where the investment is in a non-resident company, there is a requirement that the company should be subject to tax in a sovereign state in respect of its profits. Where a company would otherwise be subject to tax but for a tax holiday which the host country has granted, it will be treated, nevertheless, as satisfying this requirement.

Hong Kong is treated as a sovereign state for these purposes although its territorial basis of taxation gives rise to problems because it exempts offshore profits from taxation. The Dutch revenue authorities are understood to accept that it satisfies the second element of this requirement (ie its profits are subject to tax) where at least 50 per cent of its profits arise in Hong Kong and hence are subject to tax there. Once again it is advisable, in such circumstances, to obtain an advance ruling that the participation exemption will apply to a shareholding in a Hong Kong company.

Licensing companies

As the Netherlands grants generous tax allowances for writing off intellectual property, there has been a tendency in recent years for Dutch licensing companies to be formed which own outright the relevant intellectual property rights. The availability of tax depreciation for intellectual property rights and the use of other tax planning techniques can result in licensing income suffering a low effective rate of tax in the Netherlands. Furthermore, as the Netherlands is a signatory to the Madrid Convention, its commercial law affords these property rights considerable protection. It is thought that by owning property rights outright through a Dutch company, there is less risk of anti-treaty shopping doctrines or legislation applying to deny treaty protection to inflows of licensing income on the grounds that the company is a mere 'conduit'.

Where, on the other hand, the Dutch licensing company acts as an intermediary (or sub-licensing) company and receives royalties under the protection of the Dutch network of double tax agreements which it then pays on to a low tax or tax haven jurisdiction, an advance ruling can be obtained as to what the Dutch revenue authorities will accept as constituting an arm's length profit for the services of the Dutch company.

As a rule, the Dutch revenue authorities will regard a net profit which is equal to 7 per cent of royalties received as constituting an arm's length profit, provided that a minimum profit of Dfl 10,000 is earned. Where total royalties received exceed Dfl 2,000,000, a reduced sliding scale applies:

Dfl	%
2,000,001–4,000,000	6
4,000,001–6,000,000	5
6,000,001–8,000,000	4
8,000,001–10,000,000	3
In excess of 10,000,000	2

In the case of film royalties, a fixed 6 per cent net profit is required.

Finance companies

Because the Netherlands does not impose a withholding tax on the payment of interest, it is an attractive location in which to base a group finance company. This is especially so as inflows of interest income into such a company may benefit from the protection of the Netherlands' extensive network of double tax agreements. In order to comply with the requirements of the arm's length principle, a margin of profit must be left in charge to tax in the Dutch finance company. This margin will be determined by reference to the amount of the borrowings and will vary, depending on whether the borrowings are inter-group or external. In the case of inter-group borrowings, this margin must equal a minimum of 1/4 per cent. In the case of external borrowings, this margin will vary between 1/8 and 1/32 per cent, depending on the amount of the borrowings.

Another feature of the Dutch tax system is that where an interest-free loan is made to a Dutch company, a deduction is available in respect of interest forgone. This is based on a logical application of the arm's length principle and has been confirmed by the courts. However, the courts have further held that the interest forgone should be treated as a contribution to the capital of the Dutch company and hence will attract capital duty of 1 per cent.

Because the interest forgone will accrue to the Dutch company, although attracting little tax in the Netherlands, this arrangement is a useful means of shifting profits out of a tax haven (where they may be subject to attack under controlled foreign company legislation) or any other jurisdiction which permits the making of interest-free loans and into the Netherlands and of converting interest income into dividend income (which may escape tax in a country which applies an exemption system).

Although clearly relevant to finance company operations, such arrangements are not confined to this type of company.

Branch exemption

The profits of a foreign branch are exempt from Dutch tax where the branch is engaged in a real business activity, with sufficient substance. This exemption is granted either unilaterally or under the terms of a double tax agreement. Where granted unilaterally, there is a requirement that the branch should be subject to tax in a foreign state in respect of its income. This requirement mirrors that in relation to the participation exemption and, likewise, will be regarded as fulfilled where the branch enjoys a tax holiday.

By taking advantage of the branch exemption and investing in a foreign branch, profits can be retained in a Dutch company. This overcomes the traditional problem associated with the use of a Dutch company; namely the relatively high rates of Dutch tax which apply to profits accruing to it. A frequently encountered structure involves the use of a Swiss branch of a Dutch company. Through the use of a branch in Switzerland, both the 3 per cent Swiss capital duty and the 35 per cent Swiss withholding tax on dividends are avoided. Finance branches can obtain an almost complete tax exemption at the cantonal level. At the federal level, the Swiss revenue authorities will accept that the branch operation has a deemed debt to equity ratio of 10:1. Although Swiss federal tax is at the rate of 9.8 per cent, the availability of a deduction against branch profits for deemed interest significantly reduces the effective rate of tax which the branch suffers.

Another common structure for US multinationals involves the use of an Irish branch of a Dutch company to undertake manufacturing operations in Ireland. The profits of the Irish branch would be subject to tax in Ireland at the reduced 10 per cent rate, which is likely to be reduced to an even lower effective rate of tax because of the availability of tax allowances for capital expenditure. In the case of a US multinational, the profits of the Irish branch of the Dutch company would not be subject to attack under the Sub part 'F' provisions provided that its products underwent a substantial transformation in the manufacturing process. Where this is the case the Irish branch will benefit from the manufacturing exemption which exempts it from the provisions of Sub part 'F'.

Anti-avoidance doctrines in relation to the Netherlands/ Netherlands Antilles

Domestic anti-abuse doctrines

The Dutch Supreme Court in a decision of 8 January 1986 held that the doctrine of 'fraus legis', or abusive avoidance of tax, could be applied to the use of a Netherlands Antilles parent company as a means of avoiding Dutch withholding tax. The facts of the case involved a Canadian company which owned the shares in a Dutch company. Shortly before the Dutch company paid a dividend, the Canadian parent company reorganised its share capital and interposed a Netherlands Antilles company. When the dividend was paid to the Netherlands Antilles company, the benefit of agreement between the Netherlands and the Netherlands Antilles was claimed and the Netherlands Antilles company applied for a refund of the withholding tax. The doctrine of fraus legis was invoked to deny a full refund of the withholding tax.

Where a double tax agreement contains neither specific, nor general anti-abuse provisions, some countries may nevertheless attack conduit arrangements. The US has developed, following the *Aiken* case in 1971 (see Chapter 12: *Anti-avoidance Legislation in the International Arena*, pages 161–163 for further details), a wide range of domestic anti-treaty shopping rulings which have culminated in the incorporation of treaty override provisions in US in the 1986 Tax Reform Act.

Germany, on the other hand, upholds the principle of the sanctity of treaties in its approach to the question of treaty shopping. This issue has been considered by the courts on a number of occasions, especially in relation to the so-called 'quintet' structure. This structure involves the use of five separate holding companies to own an investment in a German company and it is employed to take advantage of the reduced rate of withholding tax granted, in a number of double tax agreements into which Germany has entered, to shareholders owning less than 25 per cent of the shares in the German company.

Specific anti-abuse provisions of certain double tax agreements

The Netherlands/Swiss treaty provides for a nil rate of withholding tax to apply to the payment of a dividend to a company which owns at least 25 per cent of the voting stock of the entity paying the dividend, provided that the relationship between the two entities has not been constituted or maintained principally for the purpose of assuring receipt of the total refund. In a decision of the Tax Court in 1982, the benefit of the full refund was denied to a Swiss company which had been incorporated by three Swiss residents. This case revolved around who should bear the burden of proof regarding the presence or absence of an intention to abuse the treaty when claiming a refund of the dividend withholding tax. The Tax Court held that this lay with the claimant and the fact that the ultimate owners of the Swiss company were themselves Swiss residents did not of itself exclude a tax avoidance motive.

Under the terms of the Netherlands/UK double tax agreement, a Dutch company which, directly or indirectly, controls 10 per cent or more of a UK company is entitled to a refund of a proportion of the tax credit available to a UK resident, individual shareholder. However, this refund is available only where the Dutch company is the beneficial owner of the shares and the ultimate ownership of the Dutch company does not lie with persons who would not themselves have benefited from this refund. Accordingly, this provision eliminates the possibility of treaty shopping.

General limitation of treaty benefits provisions

Since 1980, in all new treaty negotiations, the US has insisted on the inclusion of a general provision limiting the benefits of the treaty to bona fide residents of the treaty-partner country. Although the Dutch revenue authorities are known, in the renegotiation of the treaty between the Netherlands and the US, to have strongly resisted the inclusion of such a provision, it is thought that the new agreement will contain a general limitation of benefit provision. However, at the time of writing the terms of this agreement have not been made public. Although the new German/US double tax agreement contains a general provision limiting the benefits of the treaty, it is known that its wide scope – which has the effect of excluding residents of other EC member states from the benefit of the treaty – is a matter of concern to the European Commission who consider that it may be in breach of European law.

It is a matter of some surprise that Germany entered into a new double tax agreement with the US containing a general limitation of benefit provision of this kind as it was a signatory to a letter to the US government which argued that such a provision would be incompatible with the aim of establishing a free capital market in the EC as the 'pattern of investment relations in Europe is much more complicated than is often the case in an economy of the size of the United States, as companies in Europe often draw their capital from residents of more than one state'.

It remains to be seen whether the Dutch have been more consistent in their principles.

Conclusion

Because of its location in the heart of the European Community and the flexibility of its tax system, the Netherlands remains one of the most attractive regimes through which to structure investment. However, the growing body of international tax avoidance legislation and doctrines is increasingly circumscribing its uses. The extent of the limitation of benefits provision contained in the recently initialled US/Netherlands double tax agreement will provide an indication of how far this process has gone. Despite this, the Netherlands will remain an attractive staging post for inward investment into the European Community because European law will prevent the application of the more extreme anti-avoidance doctrines against investment from another member state.

Apart from the growth in international anti-avoidance provisions, there is growing tension in the fiscal relationship between the Netherlands and Netherlands Antilles which may culminate in an increase in the rate of withholding tax, applicable to dividend payments by Dutch subsidiaries to their Antilles parent companies.

However, the problems posed by the growth in anti-avoidance provisions and faced by the Netherlands/Netherlands Antilles are common to all such jurisdictions.

12

Anti-avoidance Legislation in the International Arena

The terms 'tax avoidance', 'tax evasion' and 'tax fraud' have slightly different connotations, depending on the jurisdiction. Whereas in some countries tax avoidance involves staying within, or possibly unintentionally straying beyond, the confines of the legally permissible, in others it is virtually synonymous with tax evasion. Although the term 'tax evasion' suggests criminality in Anglo-Saxon jurisdictions, and as such is synonymous with tax fraud, in Germany the equivalent term carries no such connotation.

However, whatever the nuances of terminology every jurisdiction will seek to protect its tax base by incorporating specific anti-avoidance provisions to cater for those eventualities which can be foreseen. For those which cannot be foreseen, most countries have a doctrine of abuse of law, abuse of form or substance over form which will allow the tax authorities to recategorise a transaction so as to deny the intended tax benefits. In some countries (eg South Africa and Australia) a general anti-avoidance provision has been incorporated into tax legislation. Regardless of whether such a provision has been incorporated into legislation or the doctrine propounded directly by the courts, the courts are likely to be the final arbiters of whether a transaction has overstepped the bounds of the permissible.

In some countries it is a moot point whether such doctrines can be applied to international transactions which involve a treaty partner. In Germany, for example, it is accepted that a treaty takes precedence over domestic law. As a consequence, domestic law may not be used to recategorise a transaction so as to deprive a resident of another country of the benefits of the treaty. This principle was established by the German Federal Court, in the so-called 'Monaco case'. In that case a resident of Monaco set up a Swiss company to hold shares in a German company. As there is no double tax agreement between Germany and Monaco, the purpose of the structure was to obtain the benefit of the reduced rate of withholding tax applicable to dividends paid by a German, to a Swiss, company. In its ruling, the court held that the establishment by a foreigner of a foreign corporation is a procedure which is outside the scope of domestic tax law and cannot therefore, as a matter of principle, be considered an abuse of forms and concepts of law (*Treaty Shopping,*

Kluwer, 1988). However, this purist view of the sanctity of treaties is not shared by many countries, least of all the US.

Anti-avoidance provisions and outward investment

The migration of companies is the ultimate means of escaping the clutches of an importunate fisc. However, the migration of a company for tax purposes will be possible only where the company law of the jurisdiction permits it and the tax legislation does not treat all locally incorporated companies as automatically resident for tax purposes. Where the tax migration of a company is feasible, the tax legislation of the country is likely to impose restrictions on such migrations. These restrictions may take the form of a requirement for an administrative consent or of a toll – or exit – charge, which involves all contingent tax liabilities crystallising at the date of migration. The UK's right to require consent from the Treasury was challenged before the European Court of Justice in the case of *R. v HM Treasury and IRC, ex parte Daily Mail and General Trust plc* on the grounds that the requirement to obtain prior consent was a breach of the Treaty of Rome as it impeded the free movement of capital within the European Community. However, the European Court rejected this argument.

Controlled foreign company legislation

The majority of developed countries have anti-avoidance legislation to prevent companies (and individuals) from obtaining tax advantages through the use of tax havens.

Where a country operates a system of worldwide taxation invariably it will permit a deferral of tax where a multinational based in its jurisdiction controls an overseas resident subsidiary which operates overseas. Thus the profits of an overseas resident subsidiary will be taxed in the jurisdiction of the parent company only when they are remitted by way of dividends. The reason for the existence of this deferral is to enable subsidiaries of its multinationals to compete on an equal footing with local companies and subsidiaries of multinationals from other jurisdictions. These other jurisdictions may operate an exemption system, under which dividends from overseas subsidiaries and the profits of overseas branches are exempt from tax in the home country, where they derive from a real business activity. However, both the exemption method and the deferral system are intended to benefit only genuine business activities.

As a consequence, most developed countries have introduced anti-avoidance legislation which is aimed either at preventing non-resident companies, over which domestic taxpayers have control or a substantial influence, from sheltering essentially passive income in a country with a significantly lower rate of tax or, in the case of a country with an exemption system, at preventing the conversion of essentially passive income into exempt dividend income receivable from a country with a low rate of tax. Although this legislation is similar in purpose, there are significant differences in the approach by various countries. For example, the French and the US legislation both seek to prevent the use of tax haven companies to avoid foreign taxes. This approach is logical in that both the deferral and the exemption method are intended to allow residents of the countries concerned to compete on equal terms with domestic investors of the host country; this neutrality would be undermined if an international investor had greater opportunity to avoid tax in the host country.

Whereas the anti-avoidance legislation of the majority of countries targets low tax countries, and then narrows its scope further by targeting only certain types of income (ie income which is not derived from a genuine business activity), the US and Canada have a different approach. Their legislation adopts a transactional approach and targets 'tainted' income, regardless of where it arises. This approach places a far greater compliance burden on taxpayers and administration alike, because it makes it necessary to track 'tainted' income, and the related overseas tax charge, at an international level.

Where a country's anti-avoidance legislation targets low tax countries, it is necessary to define a basis for determining whether a country should come within its scope. Reference to nominal rates of tax is obviously too simplistic an approach. Accordingly, the UK legislation compares the actual overseas tax charge with the equivalent UK tax charge the income would have attracted. As this definition would lead to considerable uncertainty on the part of the taxpayer, the UK publishes a list of countries which will not be regarded as low tax countries provided that any company based there derives 90 per cent or more of its income from operations within the country. A further list includes countries which will not be regarded as low tax countries where the income derived by a company does not fall into certain categories which are subject to a special, privileged, tax regime. Whereas the UK has chosen, for essentially political reasons, to list those countries which will not be regarded as low tax countries, other countries have chosen to list low tax countries. Where a so-called 'white list' of countries (ie which will not be considered as low tax countries) is issued by the revenue authorities, at least this reduces the uncertainty so far as dealings with those countries are concerned. Where, on the other hand, the revenue authorities produce a black-list of low tax countries, it provides the taxpayer with certainty only if it is an exhaustive list which is binding on the authorities. However, even where such a list is binding on the revenue authorities, the taxpayer sometimes has the right to rebut any presumption that he sought to avoid tax.

Passive, 'tainted' income invariably includes dividends, rents, royalties and interest. In addition, several countries' legislation applies to so-called base company income, ie, income deriving from related companies and/or from outside the jurisdiction in which the company is established.

Whereas some countries attribute all tainted income to domestic shareholders and tax them accordingly, others tax such income only where it exceeds a certain percentage of total income. Where domestic shareholders are subject to tax in respect of tainted income, the tax liability is calculated usually by reference to the domestic tax laws, with credit given for overseas tax already suffered.

Where countries adopt a so-called transactional approach and tax tainted income, regardless of the jurisdiction in which it arises, they may relieve nevertheless income which has already suffered a defined minimum level of overseas tax. This approach achieves a similar result to anti-avoidance legislation which targets designated tax haven jurisdictions but allows an exemption where the controlled foreign company is engaged in a bona fide commercial or industrial undertaking.

In addition to exemptions for companies carrying on bona fide commercial or industrial activity, such legislation sometimes provides other exemptions, for example:

(1) a de minimis exemption;
(2) an exemption where the controlled foreign company is quoted on a recognised overseas stock exchange;
(3) a distribution exemption. Where otherwise a company would come within the scope of anti-avoidance legislation, generally a system of worldwide taxation will grant an exemption to it if it makes an acceptable level of distributions. By distributing profits to the home country, the profits would be being brought into charge to tax and accordingly there would be no abuse of the deferral;
(4) a motive test. If the taxpayer can satisfy the revenue authorities that the reason for the existence of the controlled foreign company was not to avoid tax, the anti-avoidance legislation of some countries will not apply. This final exemption is usually a measure of last resort, with the onus of proof firmly on the taxpayer.

Under a system of worldwide taxation, anti-avoidance legislation of this type will contain detailed provisions to avoid double taxation. Otherwise this would arise where profits, which were subject to tax under controlled foreign company legislation, were remitted subsequently to the home country at which time they would attract a tax liability.

Upstream loans

A worldwide system of taxation does not tax the overseas profits which arise from a substantive business activity and accrue to an overseas resident company until the profits are remitted to the parent company by way of a dividend. Accordingly, it would be possible to avoid attracting a liability to tax by not remitting the profits by way of a dividend: instead the funds could be lent to the parent company by the overseas subsidiary. In this way, the parent company would have the use of the funds while avoiding tax on the profits. The parent company would also defer future tax to the extent that the loan generated a tax-deductible interest expense.

The US has introduced anti-avoidance provisions which have the effect of treating such loans as dividends. In 1983 the UK revenue authorities considered taxing so-called upstream loans but took a policy decision not to pursue the matter. This decision can be explained by the fact that a tax charge of this kind would have imposed a considerable one-off cost to business (in respect of existing upstream loans). In any event, the introduction of the UK's controlled foreign company legislation reduced the tax advantage arising from the deduction of the interest payable on the loan by bringing into charge to tax the corresponding interest income, where it accrued to a passive company based in a low-tax jurisdiction.

Anti-avoidance provisions affecting inward and outward investment

Transfer pricing

Countries invariably have legislation aimed at preventing the shifting of profits by an international group of companies out of their jurisdiction; so-called transfer pricing arrangements. Because companies within a group buy and sell goods and services between themselves, there is clearly scope for manipulating inter-group pricing in order to shift profits between jurisdictions. With the growth in international trade and the development of the multinational, the convention was established that these transfers should take place on the basis of arm's length prices and that overseas companies or branches should draw up separate accounts, which reflect these prices. Since the 1930s, these principles have formed the basis on which debate on issues of international tax has taken place and are the foundation on which the existing international network of double tax agreements was built.

The alternative to the arm's length principle and separate accounting was a requirement for the consolidation of the accounts of a multinational and an internationally agreed basis of formula apportionment to define the taxing rights of individual states. This would involve international agreement not only on the factors to be taken into account in any formula apportionment calculation (eg wages, capital employed etc) but also on the basis of accounting.

As separate accounting enables the taxing authorities in individual states to determine the appropriate level of a company's or branch's profits without reference to other overseas members or parts of the group, it has obvious attractions especially in a time of poor communications.

However, having embarked on that particular road and created a network of double tax agreements along the way, it now appears too late to turn back.

Despite the agreement to the arm's length principle, there was no agreement on specific rules. In 1968 the US issued regulations which sought to define specific criteria for determining the arm's length price of transactions. This was followed by the publication in 1979 of the OECD report on the issue. The OECD report adopted the same basic approach as the US regulations and recommended, in order of priority, the following methods as a means of arriving at the arm's length price:

(1) the comparable uncontrolled price: although the favoured method, it was accepted that it would be practical only where the goods were of a sufficiently common type to enable price to be readily established by reference to the price of similar goods on the market. However, this would not always be possible and, as a consequence, other methods would need to be employed;
(2) the resale price, minus an acceptable margin of profit. Where the ultimate resale price of a product is known and its price at the wholesale level needs to be established, this can be arrived at by deducting an acceptable margin of gross profit from the resale price;
(3) cost-plus method; where it is a question of determining an arm's length resale price of a product for which the costs are known, the price can be arrived at by adding a mark-up to the costs;
(4) any combination of methods (1) to (3) above.

The 1979 OECD report deliberately rejected any suggestion of a radical change of approach to this issue. However, the report did accept that 'in seeking to arrive at the arm's length price in a range of transactions, some regard to the total profits of the relevant multinational enterprise may be helpful, as a check on the assessment of the arm's length price'. It should be emphasised that this did not represent a method of arriving at an arm's length price but only a means of checking the validity of prices already established by using one of the recommended methods.

Fundamental changes in modern production processes have complicated the issues raised in the determination of an arm's length price. In particular, the fragmentation of the production process across international borders means that, instead of being required to determine the arm's length price of a single product, tax authorities are now faced with the task of determining the arm's length price of any number of components, some of which may be unique to the business. The relatively recent introduction of this new complexity has stretched the resources of revenue departments beyond breaking point; especially as an essential element of any review of the pricing policy of a group, a knowledge of the business, is often virtually the exclusive preserve of the taxpayer.

As an example of this process of fragmentation, a consumer good, eg a washing machine, may be manufactured under licence in one country, distributed to other markets from a distribution centre in another country and sold via sales companies in the countries of consumption. The patent to the washing machine design may be owned by a Swiss company and the machines may be sold under brand names that are registered in the name of a Dutch company. Furthermore, the motor incorporated into the washing machine may be manufactured separately along similar lines. This example illustrates the complexity of determining the hypothetical arm's length price in such circumstances.

The question of valuing intangibles raises a number of complex issues. For example, a research programme in pharmaceuticals will seek to develop a limited number of new products of which only some will actually come to fruition. Accordingly, it could be argued that the costs attributable to the successful product should include the costs of the unsuccessful products. Revenue authorities are concerned that taxpayers, having privileged 'inside' information, transfer the intellectual property rights in potentially successful developments into companies based in low-tax jurisdictions leaving the costs of unsuccessful developments to be borne in the high-tax jurisdiction in which the original research was undertaken. For this reason, the US Tax Reform Act of 1986 contained a provision which amended Section 482 (transfer pricing) in relation to intangibles. The amendment provides that 'in the case of any transfer (or licence) of intangible property, income with respect to such transfer or licence shall be commensurate with the income attributable to the intangible'. The so-called 'super-royalty' provision represented a legislative reversal of a previous court decision (*French v Commissioners* 1973) which held that Section 482 did not allow a long-term, fixed rate royalty agreement to be adjusted by reference to subsequent events. The same principles apply to the development of international brands, another area in which knowledge is on the side of the taxpayer.

In January 1992 the IRS issued its proposed regulations for Section 482 which provide a framework for the operation of the 'commensurate with income' provision, introduced in the Tax Reform Act of 1986. The proposed regulations lay down three methods for calculating an arm's length price for intangibles:

(1) The matching transaction method, which involves arriving at the arm's length price by obtaining the price at which an almost identical intangible has been transferred to an unrelated party. Because this method requires a very close degree of similarity between the transactions being compared, it is unlikely to be of great practical importance.
(2) The comparable adjustable transaction method. Instead of requiring the transfer of an identical intangible as a basis for comparison, this method requires a comparison between the transfer of similar

intangibles and permits larger adjustments to achieve comparability. However, this method has to be verified by applying the comparable profit interval (CPI) test, described below.
(3) The comparable profit method. This method involves calculating the transfer price by reference to a range of profits (CPI), based on the profits of comparable companies.

Because method (2) is underpinned by applying the CPI test, it is argued that it does not represent a check but that the US is proposing to adopt a de facto formula approach for the determination of transfer prices, which undermines the arm's length principle.

So far as concerns tangible property, the proposed regulations have little impact on the comparable uncontrolled price method, which remains the favoured method for determining the arm's length price. However, the use of the other three methods (resale price, cost plus and any other appropriate method) can only be used if the results obtained produce an operating income within a CPI range.

The comparable profit interval (CPI) is a range of operating profits established by reference to the profits earned by similar, independent taxpayers. The CPI is then to be applied to determine the validity of arm's length prices. However, under the current proposals, transfer prices which had been established under any method than the comparable uncontrolled price method in the case of tangible property and the matched transaction method in the case of intangible property, could be overridden where the resulting profits did not fall within the prescribed CPI range. Because the CPI test would have to be satisfied on an annual basis, companies would be required to collect data and compare their results annually with this data.

Arriving at the CPI involves a six step process which the proposed regulations define:

(1) Selecting the tested party. This will depend on a functional analysis of the business. As a rule, the tested party would have the simplest functions and the least intangibles so that extensive adjustments were not required to achieve comparability. Accordingly, the tested party would not necessarily be the US taxpayer.
(2) Determining the applicable business classification of the tested party. This will involve defining the operations to be tested and matching these with similar operations undertaken by independent parties.
(3) Computing 'constructive operating incomes'. These are computed by reference to profit level indicators for comparable businesses. These indicators may be arrived at by using ratios: in particular, the proposed regulations refer to return on assets ratio, calculations of margins and comparable profit split. Finally, any necessary adjustments would be made to the profit level indicators to arrive at constructive operating incomes (COIs).

(4) Determining the comparable profit interval. The CPI is determined by selecting the COIs which converge within a restricted range. The basis of this convergence depends on whether the COIs have been constructed from a number of profit level indicators from one independent business, or from one profit level indicator from a number of businesses.
(5) Determining the most appropriate point within the CPI. This may be determined by statistical methods, eg the mean or the median, or by reference to the most similar, independent business.
(6) Determining the transfer price. This will be the price which results in the tested party having an operating income which equates with the most appropriate point within the CPI.

Under the proposals currently before Congress (the *Rostenkowski–Gradison Bill* HR5270), the formula approach to solving the transfer pricing problem would be adopted on a more widespread basis, as a means of determining a minimum taxable income for certain foreign-owned US corporations.

Anti-avoidance provisions and inward investment

Hidden distributions

Where a payment has been made to an overseas, related party and, subsequently, the tax authorities challenge the validity of the payment, not only will they often refuse to allow a deduction of the payment for the purpose of calculating taxable profits but they will also seek to recover any withholding taxes from the paying company. Where the rate of withholding tax applicable to the payment of dividends is reduced under the terms of a double tax agreement, certain countries, notably Switzerland, will not allow this reduced rate of withholding tax to apply to a payment which was made to another group company, other than the direct parent company. Thus where interest is paid by a Swiss subsidiary to an overseas fellow subsidiary and is treated subsequently by the Swiss authorities as a hidden distribution, the favourable rate of withholding tax, which may apply to dividend payments by a subsidiary to a parent company, will not apply to such a payment (on the basis that the payment was to a fellow subsidiary and not the parent company). In the circumstances, all loans and services to a Swiss subsidiary should be provided, so far as possible, directly by the immediate parent company.

Thin capitalisation

The majority of countries' tax legislation incorporates provisions to prevent overseas investors from extracting profits out of their jurisdiction by way of excessive interest deductions. Revenue authorities in high tax countries argue that inward investors finance their operations by a disproportionate amount of borrowings, as compared with domestic investors. By financing their operations by borrowings which generate tax deductible interest expenses, they erode the country's tax base and may well enjoy a lower effective tax charge than a domestic competitor.

Accordingly most countries have introduced anti-avoidance legislation in order to limit the amount of interest which may be tax deductible in such circumstances. Generally this is framed so as to have regard to any or all of the following factors:

(1) the rate of interest;
(2) the nature of the borrowings; whether inter-group or external and, where external, whether they are secured by overseas assets of the group or supported by guarantees from group companies;
(3) the level of the company/group's capital.

So far as concerns (1), general transfer pricing rules may apply to the rate of interest on inter-group loans or, alternatively, these may be governed by anti-avoidance provisions aimed at thin capitalisation. In Switzerland, a prescribed rate of interest applies to such loans.

Where a country's thin capitalisation provisions only attack inter-group loans, they could be avoided by restructuring a group's financing arrangements so that borrowings by a company or sub-group, based in that jurisdiction, are external. Overseas assets could then be used to provide security for these borrowings or they could be supported by guarantees from group companies. For this reason, the more sophisticated anti-avoidance provisions bring within their scope external borrowings which are either secured or supported by guarantees.

Because of the difficulties involved in determining an appropriate debt/equity level for a particular type of business, certain countries prescribe a maximum debt/equity ratio which applies across the board whereas others adopt a more flexible approach and have informal safe-harbour guidelines.

However, certain methods of financing such as disguised borrowings by means of leasing or debt factoring often are not addressed by thin capitalisation provisions and may offer scope for tax planning.

Treaty shopping

Switzerland is possibly the only developed country to have introduced domestic legislation to prevent the use of its network of double tax agreements for the purpose of treaty shopping. It took this unusual step in order to allay potential treaty partners' concerns that the benefits of any treaty with Switzerland would be exploited by residents of third countries. Because rates of tax in Switzerland can be relatively low, especially in certain cantons, potential treaty partners were concerned that Switzerland would offer too great a temptation to treaty shoppers. In addition, Switzerland does not impose withholding tax on interest (except in the case of bank interest and interest on corporate bonds) or royalty payments and so profits flowing into Switzerland could be paid out, in theory at least, in this form. Where the interest and royalty payments were tax deductible in Switzerland, this structure would avoid Swiss taxation altogether.

The principal features of the Swiss Treaty Abuse decree of 1962 are that it denies the benefit of any treaty where:

(1) more than 50 per cent of income which has benefited from treaty protection is paid to non-residents by way of expenses, such as interest or royalties. This prevents income which has flowed into Switzerland under the protection of the Swiss network of double tax agreements, flowing out without incurring Swiss taxes, including withholding tax;
(2) less than 25 per cent of treaty-protected income is paid by way of dividends. By requiring at least 25 per cent of the profits to be distributed by way of dividends, Switzerland ensures that withholding tax is payable in respect of any such dividend. Where this is paid to a resident of a country which has not entered into a double tax agreement with Switzerland, the applicable rate of withholding tax is 35 per cent. However, this is reduced where there is a double tax agreement between Switzerland and the relevant country;
(3) interest bearing loans provided by non-residents may not exceed six times equity capital;
(4) the rate of interest may not exceed a rate which is prescribed from time to time by the Swiss revenue authorities.

Despite the incorporation of the Treaty Abuse decree into Swiss domestic law, a number of treaty partners have insisted nevertheless on the inclusion of specific anti-abuse provisions in their double tax agreements with Switzerland. Thus the agreements with Germany, France, Italy and Belgium incorporate provisions included in the Treaty Abuse decree with the additional requirement, in the case of royalties and interest, that where these are paid to a resident of Switzerland they should be subject to full Swiss tax (ie including cantonal taxes) in order to obtain the benefits of the agreement.

So far as concerns anti-treaty shopping measures in the host country, it is instructive to consider the body of rulings which the US has developed on this subject.

US anti-treaty shopping rulings

Revenue Ruling 84-152

Facts: a Swiss company (P) owned 100 per cent of the shares of a Netherlands Antilles company (S) and a US operating company (R). In order to finance R's working capital requirements, P lent (at 10 per cent interest) S funds which S on-lent to R (at 11 per cent interest). Although neither S nor R was thinly capitalised, S did not have sufficient funds to make the loan out of its own resources.

The ruling stated that the primary purpose for the involvement of S in the transaction was to obtain the benefit of the exemption from withholding tax under the US/Netherlands Antilles tax treaty (this has since been renegotiated and amended). Although the interest was paid directly by R to S, it was held that, because S only obtained temporary physical possession of the interest and did not obtain complete 'dominion and control' over the payments, the transaction lacked a sufficient business or economic purpose to overcome its conduit nature and, as a consequence, the benefit of the exemption under the then US/Netherlands Antilles tax treaty did not apply.

Revenue Ruling 84-153

This ruling related to a Netherlands Antilles finance subsidiary which issued bonds and lent the proceeds of the bond issue to a US subsidiary for working capital. The IRS held that the Netherlands Antilles company was merely a 'conduit' through which interest passed to the foreign bondholders as it did not have 'dominion and control' over the interest paid to it by the US subsidiary. As a consequence, the interest was subject to US withholding tax in full at the rate of 30 per cent.

Aiken Industries

The above rulings were based on the decision in the *Aiken Industries* case (1971). The facts in that case involved a Bahamian parent company (E) which had been issued with a debt instrument by its US subsidiary (M). Shortly before the interest became payable, E set up a subsidiary company (H) in Honduras to which it assigned the debt. As there was no double tax agreement between the US and the Bahamas, withholding tax of 30 per cent would have had to be withheld from the interest if it had been paid directly to E. Because there was a double tax agreement, at the time, between the US and Honduras which provided an exemption from withholding tax for interest paid by a US resident to a Honduran company, the assignment of the debt was intended to avoid the liability to withholding tax which the interest payments would have attracted if they had been paid to E. However, the Tax Court held that H had been used as a conduit for the interest payment because E had assigned the debt instrument to H only one day after its formation, for the sole purpose of obtaining the benefit of the tax treaty. As its possession of the interest had been purely temporary, it had not obtained 'dominion and control' over the funds and, as a consequence, the US/Honduras tax treaty did not apply.

Many tax practitioners thought that the implications of Rulings 84-152 and 84-153 could be avoided if the finance company subsidiary had sufficient 'substance' and obtained 'dominion and control' over any interest receipts. So far as the substance was concerned, this would involve the finance company having an office, one or two banking employees and administrative staff. It was also thought that a finance company could establish that it had 'dominion and control' over its interest receipts if these arose from its own funds. Accordingly, if the finance company was sufficiently well capitalised to be in a position to lend its own funds, there would be no requirement for it to on-pay the interest which it received and it would be impossible for the IRS to assert that it did not have 'dominion and control' over its income. However, a Technical Advice Memorandum (TAM 9133004) issued in August 1991 has cast doubt on this assumption.

Technical Advice Memorandum 9133004

The facts which form the basis for the TAM were as follows: a parent company (P) had formed an international finance subsidiary (S1) in a European country, which was an established location for such entities as it had a favourable domestic tax regime combined with an extensive network of double tax agreements. The subsidiary had significant shareholders' equity which consisted of capital contributions from the parent company and non-interest bearing convertible debentures, as well as retained earnings. Its operations also had a certain substance, with a senior international banker as its managing director, a financial controller and a secretary.

P also owned a US subsidiary (S2) which owned other US operating companies. S1 provided much of the finance for S2 and its subsidiaries. In the year under review, S1 had received capital contributions from P and had also sold convertible debentures to P and had used these funds to make two loans to S2 for an equal amount. Virtually 100 per cent of the interest received by S1 from S2 was paid by S1 to P in the form of dividends in the year of receipt.

The IRS contended that S1 was 'no less a conduit of funds because payments to P were in the form of dividends rather than interest' and justified its position by pointing to the fact that the loans made to S2 had equalled the amounts raised by S1. Furthermore the funds had been on-lent to S2 on the same day. So far as concerned the interest received, because this had been paid on to P within a short time of receipt, albeit in the form of dividends, the IRS found that S1 did not have 'dominion and control' over the interest and, as a consequence, was acting merely as a conduit. In so deciding, the IRS disregarded the fact that S1 had substantial equity as well as substance. It remains to be seen whether the IRS would be able to challenge a similar structure where a longer interval was involved between the receipt of funds and the on-lending of those same funds, as well as between the subsequent receipt of interest and its on-payment in the form of dividends.

Limitation of benefits provisions

Since 1980 in the negotiation or renegotiation of any double tax agreement, the US has sought to include a provision which limits the benefits of the agreement to 'true' residents of the treaty-partner country. Such a provision reaffirms the bi-lateral nature of the agreement and prevents treaty shopping. The recent US/German double tax agreement contains such a provision and the European Commission is understood to consider that it may contravene European law (by excluding residents of other member states from the benefit of the agreement). Although no details of the recently initialled, revised double tax agreement between the US and the Netherlands have been announced, it is thought to contain a limitation of benefits provision. It remains to be seen whether this is as all-embracing as the provision in the US/German double tax agreement or whether the reservations expressed by the European Commission have been catered for. This issue is of particular concern to UK investors, who for domestic tax reasons often own their US investments indirectly via the Netherlands. The introduction of a general limitation of benefits provision may have the effect, at worst, of denying such groups the benefit of any double tax agreement in respect of their US investments or, at best, of necessitating the possibly costly restructuring of such groups.

The inclusion of a general limitation of benefits provision in double tax agreements will have the effect of inhibiting international acquisitions as well as certain types of international reorganisations. Thus where a UK group acquires a German group with a US subsidiary, the US subsidiary will be excluded from the benefits not only of the US/German, but also of US/UK, double tax agreement.

Treaty override

A double tax treaty between two countries involves the two revenue authorities agreeing in the first instance on a ceiling for the potential tax liabilities of an investor who invests across respective borders and, secondly, on how the total tax 'take' will be shared between them. Because a double tax treaty represents an agreement between sovereign states, in the majority of countries it will take precedence over purely domestic law. However, this is not the position under US law. The US constitutional position is that a treaty is on a par with domestic legislation and, as a consequence, subsequently enacted legislation will have the effect of overriding a provision of a treaty where there is a conflict. In the past, this was not a 'live' issue because a provision was often incorporated in subsequent legislation specifically setting aside any provisions which conflicted with prior treaty obligations (eg Section 7852(d) Internal Revenue Code 1954). However, in recent years Congress has demonstrated an increasing willingness to override treaty obligations. Examples of this willingness are the introduction in 1980 of the Foreign Investment in Real Property Tax Act and the introduction of the new US branch profits tax.

In this latter example, a foreign company can retain the benefit of a reduction or elimination of these taxes under the terms of a double tax agreement but only if it can be considered a 'qualified' resident of the treaty partner country. Thus the US has introduced, unilaterally, into its domestic legislation a limitation of treaty benefits provision.

Other attempts on the part of the US at introducing specific treaty override provisions were only watered down after intensive lobbying by both governments and business interests. Congress has explicitly reserved what it regards as its right to withdraw, by legislation, benefits which have been conferred by treaty but which its treaty partner is not willing to renegotiate.

The US position on treaty override threatens to undermine the value of treaties. In developing countries treaty obligations tend to be 'more honoured in the breach than in the observance' and the US now appears to be condoning this practice.

Other measures

The majority of countries will have domestic legislation aimed at preventing tax avoidance through the exploitation at the international level of anomalies arising because of differences in countries' definition of the tax base. Examples of such domestic legislation are the restrictions imposed by the UK on tax allowances attributable to outbound leases. Before the introduction of these provisions, the UK exchequer had suffered a severe erosion of its tax take because UK financial institutions were writing an increasing amount of double-dip leases. These enabled an overseas lessee to share the benefits of the high levels of tax depreciation available to the UK financial institution through a reduction in leasing charges, while at the same time receiving the benefit of tax allowances which were due to the lessee in his country of residence.

The UK/US provisions aimed at preventing the use of dually resident companies to finance acquisitions in the other country are further examples of such anti-avoidance legislation. Because the UK/US double tax agreement does not contain a so-called 'tie-breaker' clause to determine the residence position of a company which falls within the definition of residence in both countries, it was possible so to arrange matters that a dually resident company financed any acquisition. This dually resident company (resident in the UK because that was where the company was managed and controlled, and in the US because that was where the company was incorporated, which is the primary test of corporate residence in the US) could be part of a UK tax group and, as a consequence, could obtain tax relief in the UK for its financing costs, whilst at the same time obtaining relief in the US for these same costs by virtue of its inclusion in the US consolidated filing.

There are, no doubt, a wide variety of other measures in countries' domestic legislation which aim at preventing international tax avoidance. However, these measures will have been introduced to curtail practices which seek to take advantage of specific features of a country's tax system, eg an interest deduction may be granted in one country on an accrual basis whereas the corresponding income may only be taxed in the country of receipt on the basis of the actual receipt of interest; this asymmetry could be exploited to obtain a tax deferral.

13
Conclusion

The expansion of international trade and improvements in communications have led to a growth in international tax planning. This has forced revenue authorities into responding rapidly to some of the more aggressive tax planning techniques, such as double-dip leasing, in order to stave off the threat to their tax bases. These techniques were developed originally to take advantage of opportunities offered by the interaction between two countries' tax systems and then were adapted to take advantage of any other tax system which offered a similar opportunity. Improved communication between practitioners led to an acceleration in this process and this, in turn, led to an improvement in communications between revenue authorities in the developed countries. Now, not only will the revenue authorities introduce specific anti-avoidance legislation to combat a new avoidance technique, sometimes retrospectively, but usually the courts or the legislature will have developed general anti-avoidance doctrines to cope with the unforeseen.

Developing countries have been less affected by the more sophisticated forms of international tax planning because the presence of exchange controls represents an additional line of defence against perceived abuses. The problem of dealing with a judicial system which ensures that 'the home team always wins' acts as a further deterrent, even to the adventurous. Indeed, most practitioners would be content if the majority of developing countries accepted their obligations under the terms of any double tax agreements into which they may have entered.

The growth in international trade and the mobility of capital, including production facilities, have forced countries to make their tax systems more accommodating to potential overseas investors. At one extreme, this is evidenced by the competition among tax havens to outbid one another in what has become an increasingly cut-throat business. At the other end of the spectrum, there has been a gradual alignment of tax policies among the developed countries as they have sought to broaden their tax bases and reduce their rates. There has also been a change of emphasis in tax policies, with a shift away from direct, towards indirect taxation.

However, the convergence in tax policies among developed countries and the downward pressure which this has exerted on tax rates have not led to the adoption of uniform tax systems. Although there has been a move in favour of integrated tax systems, despite their inherent bias against overseas shareholders and overseas investment, the US and the Netherlands have remained committed, until now, to a classical system. A solution to the problem of the incompatibility of tax systems will become essential if the European single market is to achieve a greater degree of economic integration among its various member states. Any solution adopted at the European level may then serve as a basis on which to address the issue in a wider, international context.

There has been a degree of convergence not only of tax rates and policies but also in the anti-avoidance legislation adopted by the major economies. Nearly all major capital exporting countries have introduced anti-avoidance provisions aimed at controlled foreign companies. By the same token, capital importing countries have strengthened their armoury of anti-avoidance provisions aimed at preventing the excessive extraction of profits through royalty and interest payments and management charges. Both capital importing and exporting countries alike have sought to reduce, if not eliminate, the transfer of profits into low tax jurisdictions by the manipulation of inter-group transfer pricing. However, because of the need of capital importing countries to attract investment, they have been reluctant to take such anti-avoidance provisions too far, for fear of driving it away.

In the past, concern at the possibility of discouraging foreign investment has not inhibited the US in the development of anti-avoidance provisions. Originally, these focused on the practice of treaty shopping; this culminated in the renegotiation of the double tax agreement with the Netherlands Antilles. At the time of its renegotiation, it was commented that the agreement with the Netherlands Antilles represented an agreement with the rest of the world (because a resident of a non-treaty country who invested in the US could always take advantage of the Netherlands Antilles' treaty to structure inward investment). For some reason, the US was reluctant to employ the anti-conduit doctrine which had been enunciated as early as 1971 in the *Aiken Industries* case. Since 1980, the US has sought instead to include a limitation of benefits provision in any new double tax agreement which it concludes, or any existing agreement which it renegotiates. In this way the US has sought to reaffirm the bilateral nature of double tax agreements. Despite the UK's objection to the principle of such limitation of benefits provisions, it is noteworthy that the recent draft UK/Denmark double tax agreement contains such a provision in relation to interest and royalty payments and that this was introduced at the insistence of the UK negotiating team. Member states of the European Community have also introduced similar provisions when incorporating into their domestic legislation the European parent/subsidiary directive, abolishing withholding taxes on payments of dividends by subsidiaries to a parent company in another member state.

Provisions which limit the availability of treaty benefits in this way can have the effect of impeding international acquisitions or the reconstruction of groups. For example, a UK-based group which acquires a German group with a US subsidiary, will find that the US subsidiary cannot benefit from the double tax agreement between the US and Germany (because ultimate ownership lies in the UK) and yet will not be able to benefit from the US/UK double tax agreement. Thus a group in this position will be deprived of the benefit of any double tax agreement in relation to its investment in the US.

As industrial policy of the European Community aims to encourage Pan-European mergers and reconstructions, limitation of benefits provisions place a serious obstacle in the way of its realisation. It is for this reason that the recently initialled double tax agreement between the US and the Netherlands is rumoured (incorrectly, as subsequent publication has proved) to contain a limitation of benefit provision which does not deny the benefit of the agreement where the ultimate ownership of a Dutch company lies with residents of other member states. However, it remains to be seen whether a provision such as this, which accepts by implication the wider economic integration of the European Community, gains acceptance and becomes a model for the future.

Apart from reaffirming their bilateral nature by seeking to include a limitation of benefits provision in all its double tax agreements, the US is threatening to undermine the value of any such agreements by the frequent recourse to treaty override provisions in its domestic legislation. No purpose is served by having an agreement if one of the parties does not regard itself as being bound by its terms.

The emergence of trading blocs not only puts under strain the essentially bilateral network of double tax agreements, but it also raises issues relating to the domestic tax systems of overseas investors investing in the trading bloc. Thus the US sub part 'F' legislation defines as objectionable certain activities which are the inevitable and intended consequences of the economic integration of the European Community. For example, production will be rationalised and concentrated in a limited number of member states; likewise, distribution and administration will become more focused, leaving skeleton sales operations to service the markets of individual member states. This reduction in the substantive activities undertaken within certain member states is precisely what anti-avoidance legislation of the sub part 'F' variety targets as an abuse of the tax deferral, generally permitted by a system of worldwide taxation.

Another source of instability in the international tax environment has arisen from the threat, posed by a number of American states, to the arm's length principle. This threat arises from the introduction of so-called unitary tax as an alternative to taxing those profits which are reflected in the accounts of the business and which arise within their jurisdiction. These accounts would be drawn up to reflect the inter-group pricing of goods and services on the basis of a hypothetical arm's length price. By contrast, under a unitary system of taxation the profits of unitary businesses are combined and the taxable profits are then determined by reference to a formula calculation.

Originally the unitary tax system applied to divide profits of a multistate corporation or business between the various states. In 1872 Illinois introduced a state railroad tax which attributed the tax to each county, city or town by reference to the length of track within the locality, compared with the total length of track. With the internationalisation of businesses, it only required a small step for states to extend this basis of taxation to apply to the worldwide profits of multinational companies.

Unitary tax applies to businesses which have unity of operation, management and ownership. Where these three unities are present, a multinational group will be required to provide a combined report, covering its worldwide operations, for the purpose of applying the necessary formula calculation to determine how much of its profits are subject to state tax. This combined report has to be drawn up according to US accounting conventions. The resulting net profit may be subject to further adjustment to arrive at the income relating to the unitary business to which the formula calculation applies. In the case of Californian unitary tax, this formula compares property, payroll and sales within and outside California. Not only does the requirement to recompute profits in this way impose a considerable compliance cost on the groups affected, but, if this basis of taxation were to spread, it would undermine the arm's length principle which underlies the network of double tax agreements built up since the end of the Second World War.

Because of the concern that unitary tax may lead to the adoption of a formula approach by other countries (and not just by political sub-divisions) business interests mounted a concerted lobbying campaign against the principle of unitary tax. This campaign won the support of a number of governments, which sought to protect their investors from this form of taxation by including in any renegotiated double tax agreement with the US a provision excluding the application of such a tax. The UK had sought to obtain protection for its investors along these lines, when it sought to include within Article 9 (relating to the arm's length principle) a new clause 4 which would have excluded the application by any US state of any basis of taxation which departed from the arm's length principle. However, the US Senate refused to ratify the treaty until this particular clause was removed. The Senate's objection was on the grounds that this clause was unconstitutional because it represented federal interference in the states' constitutional right to tax. Although the possibility of obtaining protection from unitary taxation through double tax agreements now appears remote, business lobbying was successful in persuading states to restrict unitary tax to the 'water's edge' approach, as opposed to the previous worldwide basis. However, the constitutionality of unitary tax continues to be challenged in the US courts on the basis that the extraterritoriality involved in worldwide unitary tax interferes with the Federal Government's constitutional right to conduct foreign affairs. There is every likelihood that the case will provide a good living, beyond the foreseeable future, to the lawyers working on it.

Throughout the unitary tax debate, the concern of the business sector has been that undermining the arm's length principle, without an agreed, alternative basis to put in its place, would lead to double taxation as countries, in defining their tax bases, adopted incompatible formula calculations and applied these to combined or consolidated accounts drawn up under differing conventions. Having maximised their own income, the multinationals would then be left to shoulder the resulting burden of double taxation.

Although this concern originally focused on developing countries, who it was feared would emulate the US example and adopt a formula apportionment basis of taxing profits as a means of increasing their revenue yield, the main threat to the arm's length principle appears to come once again from the US, except this time it comes from the Federal, and not the state governments. This new threat took the form of proposed regulations relating to transfer pricing, in which the concept of the comparable profit interval was introduced as a method of arriving at the transfer price; see Chapter 12: *Anti-avoidance Legislation in the International Arena*, pages 157–159. This method was based, in effect, on a formula apportionment calculation and, whereas the OECD report on transfer pricing had countenanced the use of a calculation along such lines as a check on the validity of transfer prices, which had been determined on the basis of the arm's length principle and in accordance with guidelines laid down by the OECD, the US proposed method was intended to override these in the majority of cases. A further threat came from the *Rostenkowski–Gradison Bill* put before Congress, which proposed the imposition of a minimum tax, once again based on a formula apportionment calculation, on foreign-owned businesses operating in the US. Although this provision has been removed from the Bill, and it is understood that the comparable profit interval is to have a reduced importance in the final US regulations on transfer pricing, the outlook of the US tax environment remains ominous.

Whereas in the past tax savings were readily available by putting in place the structures outlined in this book, now these savings are available on only a very selective basis, having been eroded by the growth of 'copycat' anti-avoidance legislation. Increasingly groups are looking to minimise their exposure to risk, rather than for windfall profits, which may depend on putting in place a long-term structure which may in the event prove to have only a limited life.

In order to minimise risks, it should be borne in mind that a chain is only as strong as its weakest link and, inevitably, a complex series of transactions will be vulnerable to attack at a number of points.

Accordingly, it is important to strive for simplicity when structuring a group or its activities.

Apart from trying to limit the number of steps in a transaction, it is important at an international level to limit the number of jurisdictions through which a transaction passes. The reason for this is that almost every jurisdiction will want to tax, in one form or another, any profit arising on a transaction which passes through it. As a consequence, the greater the number of countries through which profits flow, the greater the likelihood of their erosion through taxation. Even where the passage of the profits is protected by a network of double tax agreements, these have become subject to such frequent change that it would be unwise to place too great a faith in them. Furthermore, where profits benefit from an exemption or other privileged treatment in a particular jurisdiction, there is always the danger that the domestic legislation will be amended and the favourable treatment withdrawn. This is clearly a greater risk in a high tax jurisdiction which, by definition, has committed itself to the principle of taxation. By contrast, a tax haven which has built up a financial sector by holding out the prospect of low or nil taxes is unlikely to break faith with investors, as this would serve only to undermine confidence in its financial sector.

A global recession may dispel the prospect of countries attracting significant, additional inward investment. As stated previously, it was this prospect which caused exchequers to exercise self-restraint in the past. With its disappearance, the inevitable political consequence will be that the foreign investment, which was previously welcomed, will be seen increasingly as a source of additional revenue. This could lead ultimately to a new era of covert expropriation of foreign investment via the tax system, with the measures dressed up as anti-avoidance legislation in order to restrict debate to a technical level and keep it outside the public forum.

It remains to be seen whether the European Community can unite to avert this threat to its outward investment or whether the deep political divisions within Europe will mean that instead member states vie with one another to make their (unharmonised) tax systems more accommodating to potential inward investors. The Dutch tax system combined with Irish manufacturing relief offers an ideal combination for the inward investor, especially where the business operations are capital intensive with high value added.

In order to respond to this threat, practitioners need to ensure that the groups which they are advising are conservatively structured and that the more aggressive planning techniques are short term in nature, so as not to create a possible ongoing exposure. The use of financial instruments and hedging techniques provides a means of achieving one-off benefits of this kind.

It should be remembered that tax is a business cost and, because the rates, base and system are determined by governments, the management of a business has control over only limited aspects of this cost. Because of its specialised nature, control of the tax function has been passed to specialists. This, combined with the fact that management is traditionally judged on the basis of profits before tax, has contributed to the marginalisation of the tax function within businesses. This process has been reinforced by the often introverted nature of practitioners who are attracted to this area of specialisation. This marginalisation of the tax function helps explain businesses' failure to appreciate the significance of the storm clouds which are gathering on the US horizon.

Appendix I

Tax systems, basis of taxation of foreign income, interest relief for overseas investment.

Country	Tax system	Basis of taxation of foreign source dividend income	Interest relief foreign income
EC Member States:			
Belgium	classical	exemption	available
Denmark	partial imputation	exemption	restricted
France	partial imputation	exemption	restricted
Germany	split rate/full implication	exemption	restricted
Greece	dividend deduction	credit by source	restricted
Ireland	partial imputation	credit by source	available
Italy	full imputation	credit by source	restricted
Luxembourg	classical	exemption	restricted
Netherlands	classical	exemption	restricted
]Portugal	partial shareholder relief	credit by source	restricted
Spain	partial imputation	credit by source	restricted
United Kingdom	partial imputation	credit by source	available
Australia & Far East:			
Australia	full imputation	exemption	restricted
Hong Kong	full shareholder relief	exemption	restricted
Japan	partial shareholder relief	worldwide credit	available
Malaysia	full imputation	credit by source	restricted
Singapore	full imputation	credit by source	restricted
America:			
United States	classical	worldwide	restricted
Canada	partial shareholder relief	exemption	restricted

Appendix II

Table 1. Total tax revenue as a percentage of gross domestic product at market prices:

	1989
Denmark	49.9
Netherlands	46.0
Belgium	44.3
France	43.8
Luxembourg	42.4
Germany	38.1
Italy	37.8
Ireland	37.6
United Kingdom	36.5
Portugal	35.1
Spain	34.4
Greece	33.2

Table 2. Tax revenue of main headings as percentage of total taxation.

	Income & Profits	*Social Security*	*Payroll*	*Goods & Services*	*Property*	*Other*
Belgium	37.6	34.2		25.5	2.7	
Denmark	59.5	2.4	0.6	33.0	4.3	0.2
France	17.4	43.9	1.9	28.7	5.0	3.1
Germany	35.0	36.3		25.6	3.1	
Greece	18.3	31.6	1.7	45.0	3.4	
Ireland	35.1	14.5	1.3	44.3	4.8	
Italy	37.1	33.2	0.5	26.9	2.3	
Luxembourg	41.1	26.2		24.4	8.3	
Netherlands	28.8	41.0		26.1	3.8	0.3
Portugal	26.4	26.3		45.1	1.5	0.7
Spain	32.9	34.6		28.7	3.8	
United Kingdom	38.9	17.6		30.9	12.6	

Source: OECD Revenue Statistics 1991 (Reproduced with permission)

Appendix III

Dutch Network of Double Tax Agreements –
Income flows to and from the Netherlands

Withholding tax rates applicable to:
(in the case of dividends only the rate applicable to substantial shareholdings and the relevant definition – is shown)

		Income receivable by a Dutch company			**Dividend* payments**
	Substantial holdings	**Dividend**	**Royalty**	**Interest**	
Austria	–	–	10	10	0
Australia	25	10/0	0/10	0	0
Belgium	25	5	0	0	0
Canada	25	10	0/15	15	10
China (People's Republic)	–	10	10	10	10
Czechoslovakia	25	0	5	0	0
Denmark	25	0	–	–	0
Finland	25	0	0	0	0
France	25	5	0	0/10	0
Germany	25	25	0	0/15	0
Greece	–	–	7/10	8/10	5
Hungary	25	5	–	–	5
India	–	15	20	15	15
Indonesia	25	10	5/20	10/20	0
Ireland	–	–	0	0	0
Israel	–	15	5/10	10/15	5
Italy	75	0	0	15/20	0
Japan	25	10	10	0/10	5
Korea (South)	25	10	10/15	10/15	10
Luxembourg	25	0	0	0	0
Malaysia	–	–	10	0/15	0
Malta	–	–			5
Morocco	25	10			10
Netherlands Antilles	–	–	–	–	5/7.5
New Zealand	–	15	10	10	15
Norway	–	15	–	–	0
Pakistan	25	10	5/15	15/20	10
Philippines	10	10	10/15	10/15	10
Poland	25	0	0/10	0	0
Romania	25	10	10	0/10	10
Singapore	–	–	0/30	10	0
South Africa	25	5	0	10	5
Spain	50	10	6	10	5
Sri Lanka	25	15	10	5/10	10
Surinam	25	7.5/15	5	10	7.5/15
Sweden	25	0	0	–	0
Switzerland	25	0	–	0/5	0
Thailand	25	10	5/15	10/20	5
Turkey	25	15	10	10/15	15
United Kingdom	5	10	0	0	0
United States+	25	5	0	0	5
Yugoslavia	25	5	10	0	5
Zambia	25	5	10	0	5
Zimbabwe	25	10	10	10	10

+ new agreement initialled.
* substantial shareholding is 25 per cent, except where indicated by X when a lower level applies

Bibliography

The following bibliography is only a selective list of some of the more important contributions to the subject matter. A more comprehensive bibliography is contained in International Business Taxation (see below).

Journals:

In order to keep abreast of developments, readers are recommended to subscribe to a good quality journal on the subject. Highly recommended is:

- Tax Planning International Review. Published in the UK by BNA International Inc.

Books and Articles:

- International Business Taxation – Weidenfeld paperbacks, Sol Piccciotto (1992).
- Finance, Investment and Taxation Decisions of Multinationals – Basil Blackwell, J.S. Alworth (1988).
- OECD. Taxing profits in a global economy (1991).
- Trends in International Taxation – IBFD, David W. Williams (1991).
- The International Taxation of Multinational Enterprises in Developed Countries – Associated Business Programs, Adams J.R.D. & Whalley J. (1977).
- Double Taxation Agreements and International Tax Law – Sweet & Maxwell, P. Baker (1991).
- Principles of International Double Taxation Relief – Sweet & Maxwell, David R. Davies (1985).
- International Tax Treaty Service – In-depth Publishing Company, M. Edwards – Ker.
- OECD (1977) Model Double Taxation Convention on Income and Capital.
- OECD (1992) Model Double Taxation Convention on Income and Capital.
- Corporate Tax Harmonisation and Economic Efficiency – Institute for Fiscal Studies (Report 35, 1989), Michael Devereux and Mark Pearson.
- Removal of Tax Obstacles to the Cross Frontier Activities of Companies – Bulletin of the European Supplement 4/91.

– Conclusions and Recommendations of the Committee of Independent Exports on Company Taxation. Commission of the European Communities (ISBN 92–826–3990–8).

– Report of the Committee of Independent Experts on Company Taxation (full text). Commission of the European communities (ISBN 92–826–4277–1).

– Company Tax Harmonisation in the European Community – Institute of Directors 1989, J.F. Chown.

– Tax Havens Encyclopaedia – Butterworths, Editor Barry Spitz.

– U.S. Department of Treasury Reports:
Tax havens and their uses by United States Taxpayers: An Overview (1981).

– Tax Havens in the Caribbean basin (1981).

– The Taxation of Controlled Foreign Companies – Canadian Tax Foundation (1986), Brian J. Arnold.

– Tax Avoidance, Tax Evasion – Sweet & Maxwell (1984) – International Bar Association.

– Treaty Shopping – Kluwer Law and Taxation Publishers (1988), Deloitte Haskins & Sells.

– International Tax Avoidance and Evasions: Four related studies OECD (1987).

– Transfer Pricing and Multinational Enterprises – OECD (1979).

– Transfer Pricing and Multinational Enterprises Three Taxation Issues – OECD (1984).

– Tax Efficient Foreign Exchange Management – Woodhead – Faulkner Ltd, J.F. Chown.

– Company Reorganisations – Butterworths (1990) Tomsett and Noble.

– Imputation systems – an overview
Journal of Strategy in International Taxation
volume 4 number 1, J.F. Chown.

– Demise off the equity wall – Tax planning International Review (January 1992), Michael S. Lebovitz.

– Hong Kong and Singapore as regional headquarter centres. – Journal of strategy in International Taxation volume 4 number 2, A.E. Ogley.

– The Joy of Imputation – Tax Journal (May 1989), S. Edge.

– Income Tax Arrangements – Tax Journal (August 1989) – F.G. Sandison.

– Stapled Stock: Is it as easy as it sounds – Tax Journal (March 1991).

– Combining US and UK corporations: Tax lawyer (Vol. 42 1989), P.C. Canellos.

– Cahiers de droit fiscal IFA, in particular Vol. LXXVa on leasing.

Index